THE BATTLES OF WILDERNESS & SPOTSYLVANIA

CIVIL WAR SERIES

TEXT BY GORDON C. RHEA

Maps by George Skoch

Thanks to Robert Krick and Donald Pfanz at Fredericksburg and Spotsylvania National Military Park.

Published by Eastern National, copyright 1995.

Eastern National provides quality educational products and services to America's national parks and other public trusts.

Cover: Sixth Corps Skirmishers in the Wilderness, by Julien Scott. Courtesy of Robert A. McNeil.

Back cover: Lee's Texans by Don Troiani. Courtesy of Historical Art Prints, Ltd., Southbury, CT.

Printed on recycled paper.

THE BATTLES OF WILDERNESS & SPOTSYLVANIA

During the winter of 1863–1864, the Union Army of the Potomac and the Confederate Army of Northern Virginia faced each other across the Rapidan River in central Virginia. The Union forces, commanded by Major General George G. Meade, were quartered around Culpeper Court House. The Confederates, led by General Robert E. Lee, were camped around Orange Court House. Clark's Mountain, a prominent ridge on the river's southern bank, served as a lookout station for the rebels. The conical tents of Meade's army were clearly visible on the fields below.

The spring of 1864 opened the Civil War's fourth year. In March, Ulysses S. Grant—hero of Vicksburg and Chattanooga—was elevated to the rank of lieutenant general and placed in command of all Union armies in hope that he would bring unity to the Federal war effort. Grant decided to make his headquarters with the Army of the Potomac. He was to concentrate on general strategy while his

army commanders—including Meade—managed their forces and tended to tactical matters.

Grant planned to attack Lee from three directions. First, the Army of the Potomac, augmented by Major General Ambrose E. Burnside's Ninth Corps, was to cross the Rapidan east of Lee, flanking the rebels out of their strong earthworks along the Rapidan. Once over the river, Meade was to swing west and engage Lee in battle. At the same time, a second army under Major General Benjamin Butler was to depart from its camps at Fort Monroe and advance up the James River toward Richmond. Grant hoped that Butler would either capture the Confederate capital or, if that proved impossible, wait for Meade. Finally, a third Federal army under Major General Franz Sigel was to advance south through the Shenandoah Valley, menacing Lee's left flank and disrupting his supplies.

Lee had no choice but to assume a defensive posture. Meade's and Burnside's

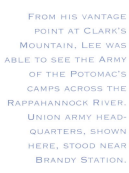

FROM HIS VANTAGE POINT AT CLARK'S MOUNTAIN, LEE WAS ABLE TO SEE THE ARMY OF THE POTOMAC'S CAMPS ACROSS THE RAPPAHANNOCK RIVER. UNION ARMY HEADQUARTERS, SHOWN HERE, STOOD NEAR BRANDY STATION.

(BL)

juggernaut numbered some 120,000 men, compared to Lee's 65,000 soldiers. And while the Federal hosts were well provisioned and supplied, Lee's veterans labored under deficiencies in food, clothing, and weapons.

In order to meet Grant's expected onslaught, Lee left Lieutenant General Richard S. Ewell's Second Corps and Lieutenant General Ambrose P. Hill's Third Corps behind earthworks along the Rapidan. Lieutenant General James Longstreet's First Corps meanwhile waited in the rear at Gordonsville, from where it could reinforce the Rapidan works or shift to Richmond, depending on how matters developed. Lee's cavalry under Major General James Ewell Brown "Jeb" Stuart patrolled the countryside past the ends of the Rapidan line. It was Lee's hope that his scouts and cavalry would alert him in time to respond once Grant revealed his intentions.

MAY 4: THE CAMPAIGN OPENS

Meade had the Army of the Potomac in motion well before daylight on May 4 to steal a march on Lee. The Federals

advanced in two columns, each preceded by cavalry. One wing, consisting of Major General Gouverneur K. Warren's Fifth Corps and Major General John Sedgwick's Sixth Corps, crossed on pontoon bridges at Germanna Ford. Major General Winfield Scott Hancock's Second Corps crossed a few miles east at Ely's Ford. By noon, Hancock's men were settling into camps at Chancellorsville. Warren's troops continued about five miles below the river to Wilderness Tavern, where Orange Turnpike struck Germanna Plank Road, and Sedgwick's corps occupied the road back to Germanna Ford.

Grant and Meade camped on a knoll near Wilderness Tavern. Nearby was Ellwood, home of the Lacy family, that served as Warren's headquarters. Grant expressed relief that the army had crossed the Rapidan without incident. He planned to continue his maneuver toward Lee the next morning, with Warren cutting over to Orange Plank Road and bivouacking near Parker's Store, Sedgwick occupying Warren's former camp at Wilderness Tavern, and Hancock proceeding west along Catharpin Road until he reached a point roughly south of Warren. The delay would give Burnside time to arrive. By

A TRAIN OF 4,300 WAGONS FOLLOWED THE UNION ARMY INTO THE WILDERNESS. IF PLACED END TO END, THE WAGONS WOULD HAVE STRETCHED A DISTANCE OF 60 MILES —FROM THE RAPIDAN RIVER TO RICHMOND.

(LC)

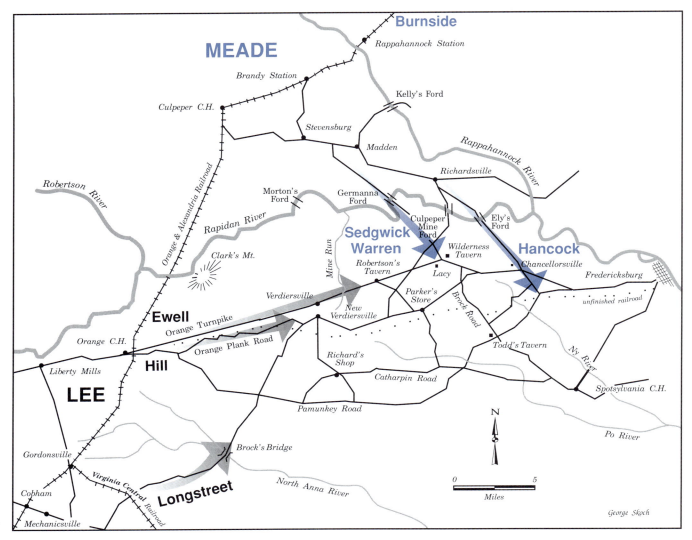

THE ARMIES MARCH INTO THE WILDERNESS: MAY 4

On May 4, the Army of the Potomac crosses the Rapidan River at Germanna and Ely's Fords, entering the area known as the Wilderness, leaving Burnside's Ninth Corps to guard the Orange and Alexandria Railroad. Lee moves east to intercept Grant in the Wilderness, sending Ewell's corps down the Orange Turnpike and A. P. Hill's corps down the Orange Plank Road. Longstreet's corps, camped near Gordonsville, hastens toward the battlefield by way of Brock's Bridge.

noon, Grant expected to be drawn up in a line roughly north to south and oriented toward Lee.

Two miscalculations, however, marred Grant's plan. First, by halting early on May 4, the Union army was forced to camp overnight in the Wilderness of Spotsylvania. The area had been stripped of trees during colonial times and later to provide fuel for smelting operations, and by 1864, thick stands of second-growth forest blanketed the region. If Grant tried to fight there, he would lose many of his advantages. Artillery and cavalry were

useless and infantry maneuvers virtually impossible. "This, viewed as a battle ground, was simply infernal," a Union staffer remarked. Meade, however, recommended spending the night in the Wilderness to give the army's wagons time to catch up.

Grant's second miscalculation was that Lee could not reach the Wilderness before late on May 5. Acting on that assumption, Meade neglected to ensure that the roads toward Lee were adequately patrolled. Brigadier General James H. Wilson, whose cavalry division was charged with protecting the army's western flank, failed to leave pickets on Orange Turnpike, opening the way for a surprise attack by Lee.

By noon on the fourth, Lee had reacted to the Federals swarming over the Rapidan. Ewell's corps filtered from its Rapidan entrenchments to Orange Turnpike and marched toward the Wilderness. That night Ewell's lead units reached Robertson's Tavern and bedded down within three miles of Warren's unsuspecting troops. Hill's corps meanwhile advanced in tandem with Ewell's along Orange Plank Road and stopped at the hamlet of New Verdiersville. Around 4:00 P.M., Longstreet started from Gordonsville toward the Wilderness by a more southerly route.

During the night, Stuart's scouts confirmed that Grant was still in the Wilderness. Lee decided to attack right

away. At first light, Ewell was to push along the turnpike toward Grant while Hill continued east on the Plank Road. The two corps were to pin Grant in place until Longstreet could arrive and slam into Grant's exposed southern flank. Lee was a bold strategist, and he was counting on the Wilderness to help neutralize Grant's numbers. But Lee's was a dangerous scheme. To succeed, he would have to immobilize Grant's entire force for a day with fewer than 40,000 men, and Longstreet would have to arrive precisely as planned.

May 5: Ewell Surprises Warren on Orange Turnpike

Early on the morning of May 5, the Union Fifth Corps started out a farm path toward Orange Plank Road, leaving pickets a short way out Orange Turnpike to sound the alarm if Confederates came from that direction. As the pickets prepared to move

on, they saw a wisp of dust on the horizon. Soon Ewell's corps appeared, marching straight toward the enemy.

Warren sent word to Meade that Confederates were approaching. The army commander in turn notified Grant, who directed that "if any opportunity presents itself of pitching into a part of Lee's army, do so without giving time for disposition." Assuming that the unexpected gray-clad visitors constituted only a small body, Meade halted his army and directed Warren to attack.

The Confederates began erecting earthworks along the western edge of a

clearing known as Saunders Field. Warren advanced Brigadier General Charles Griffin's division to the east edge of the clearing. Brigadier General James S. Wadsworth's division formed in dense woods on Griffin's left, and Brigadier General Samuel W. Crawford's Pennsylvania Reserves occupied the Chewning farm knoll farther south. Warren hesitated to attack, however, because the Confederate formation overlapped Griffin's flank and would enfilade him if he advanced. Warren beseeched Meade to postpone the assault until Sedgwick arrived and formed on his right. By 1:00 P.M., however, Meade had become so exasperated with Warren's delay that he ordered him to proceed without Sedgwick. "It was afterwards a common report in the army," an aide recounted, "that Warren had just had unpleasant things said to him by General Meade, and that

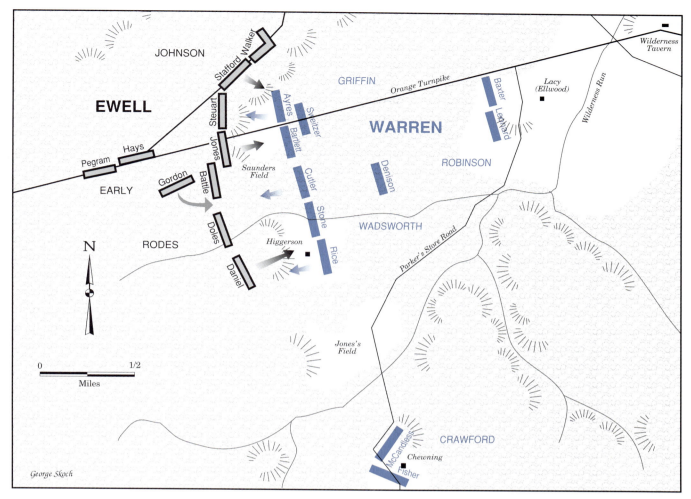

WARREN OPENS THE FIGHTING: MAY 5, 1:00 P.M.
Griffin attacks Ewell across Saunders Field, supported by Wadsworth's division south of the turnpike. The Federals
succeed in rupturing the center of Ewell's line below the road, but vigorous counterattacks by John Gordon, Junius
Daniel and others quickly restore the line. To the south, Crawford's division maintains its hold on the Chewning
farm, while two brigades of Robinson's division remain in reserve near the Lacy House.

General Meade had just heard the bravery of his army questioned."

Griffin's men strode across Saunders Field into intense Confederate firepower. Brigadier General Romeyn B. Ayres's brigade, on Griffin's right, was blistered by Southerners shooting from behind earthworks to the front and right. Blue-clad survivors broke across the field, many seeking refuge in a gully. Brigadier General Joseph J. Bartlett, advancing up the turnpike's left side, had slightly better success. His lead units overran the Confederate line—commanded by Brigadier General John M. Jones, who was killed—and punched forward about a quarter of a mile. Ayres's

inability to keep pace, however, left Bartlett's rightmost flank exposed, and rebels quickly exploited the weak point. Bartlett fled with his men and barely escaped capture when his horse was shot from under him.

Brigadier General Lysander Cutler's famed Iron Brigade advanced in tandem with Bartlett through woods immediately south of Saunders Field. Although Cutler initially made headway against Brigadier General Cullen A. Battle's Alabamians, he was brought up short by a counterattack launched by Brigadier General John B. Gordon. Positioned near the turnpike, the charismatic Gordon thrust his brigade into

"SURRENDER OR DIE!"

The dense woods of the Wilderness made possible surprises and in many instances fostered panic among the troops who fought there. A case in point is the experience of Lieutenant Holman Melcher of the Twentieth Maine Volunteers. On May 5, Warren's Fifth Corps broke Ewell's line south of the Orange Turnpike, driving the Confederates back half a mile. Melcher and a small body of men plunged through the break and when Ewell successfully counterattacked, they found themselves trapped behind enemy lines. Faced with the alternative of being sent to a Confederate prison camp, they boldly determined to cut their way out. Melcher described the episode in a speech delivered to the Military Order of the Loyal Legion a quarter-century after the battle.

"As we emerged from the woods into this field, General Bartlett, our brigade commander, came galloping down the line from the right, waving his sword and shouting, 'Come on, boys, let us go in and help them!' And go we did. Pulling our hats low down over our eyes, we rushed across the field, and overtaking those of our comrades who had survived the fearful crossing of the front line, just as they were breaking over the enemy's lines, we joined with them in this deadly encounter, and there in that thicket of bushes and briers, with the groans of the dying, the shrieks of the wounded, the terrible roar of musketry and the shouts of command and cheers of encouragement, we swept them away before us like a whirlwind . . . .

The pursuit of my company and those immediately about me continued for about half a mile, until there were no rebels in our front to be seen or heard; and coming out into a little clearing, I thought it well to reform my line, but found there was no line to form, or to connect it with. I could not find my regimental colors or the regiment. There were with me fifteen men of my company with two others of the regiment. I was the only commissioned officer there, but my own brave and trusted first sergeant, Ammi Smith, was at my side as always in time of danger or battle, and with him I conferred as to what it was best to do under the circumstances.

There was nothing in front to fight that we could see or hear, but to go back seemed the way for cowards to move, as we did not know whether our colors were at the rear or farther to the front. I was twenty-two years old at this time, and Sergeant Smith twenty-three, so that our united ages

the head of Cutler's advance, then spread units right and left to chew their way through the Federal formation. For the first time in its history, the Iron Brigade broke and streamed rearward. On Cutler's left, Colonel Roy Stone's Pennsylvanians entered dense woods bordering the Higgerson place. They mired in a swamp —the "champion mud hole of mud holes," a survivor described it—while Brigadier General George Doles's Georgians fired into them from a nearby ridge. To the left of Stone, Brigadier General James C. Rice's brigade crossed a clearing, became disoriented in a stand of woods, and fled as Brigadier General Junius Daniel's North Carolinians emerged from the thickets onto its flanks.

As the Union formation dissolved, Crawford began hurrying his division back. One regiment—the Seventh Pennsylvania —became separated and was captured by a handful of Gordon's Georgians under Major Frank Van Valkenberg. Under cover of the dense woods, the Georgia major was able to make his squad appear as though it were a regiment. "I never saw a group of more mortified men," a Southerner remarked of the Pennsylvanians' reaction on discovering they had been tricked into surrendering to a vastly inferior force.

hardly gave years enough to decide a question that seemed so important to us at that moment . . . .

Forming our 'line of battle' (seventeen men beside myself) in single rank, of course . . . we approached quietly and unobserved, as the 'Johnnies' were all intent on watching for the 'Yanks' in front, not for a moment having a suspicion that they were to be attacked from the rear, until we were within ten or fifteen paces, when on the first intimation that we were discovered, every one of our little band picked his man and fired, and with a great shout as much as if we were a thousand, we rushed at them and on to them, sword and bayonets being our weapons. 'Surrender or die!' was our battle-cry.

They were so astonished and terrified by this sudden and entirely unexpected attack and from this direction, that some of them promptly obeyed, threw down their arms and surrendered. The desperately brave fought us, hand to hand; the larger part broke and fled in every direction through the woods, and could not be followed by us or our fire, as our rifles were empty and there was no

time to reload.

This was the first, and I am glad to say, the last time that I saw the bayonet used in its most terrible and effective manner. One of my men, only a boy, just at my side, called out to a rebel to throw down his gun, but instead of obeying he quickly brought it to his shoulder and snapped it in the face of this man, but fortunately it did not explode, for some reason.

Quick as a flash, he sprang forward and plunged his bayonet into his breast, and throwing him backward pinned him to the ground, with the very positive remark, 'I'll teach you, old Reb, how to snap your gun in my face!' And this was only one scene of many such I saw enacted around me, in that terrible struggle. How I wished my sword had been ground to the sharpness of a razor, but the point was keen and I used [it] to the full strength of my arm.

I saw a tall, lank rebel, only a few paces from me, about to fire at one of my men and I the only one that could help him. I sprang forward and struck him with all my strength, intending to split his head open, but so anxious was I that my blow should fall on him

before he could fire that I struck before I got near enough for the sword to fall upon his head, but the point cut the scalp on the back of his head and split his coat all the way down his back. The blow hurt and startled him so much that he dropped his musket without firing and surrendered, and we marched him out with the other prisoners.

In less time than it has taken me to tell this we had scattered the line of battle and the way was open for us to escape. Two of our little band lay dead on the ground where we had fought, and several more or less severely wounded, but these latter we kept with us and saved them from capture. By spreading our little company out rather thin we were able to surround the thirty-two prisoners we had captured in the melee and started them along on the double quick, or as near to it as we could and keep the wounded along with us.

The Confederate line soon began to rally and fired after us; but as there were many more of the Gray than the Blue in our ranks, they hesitated to do much firing, as they saw they would be more likely to kill friends than foes."

"There was nothing in front to fight that we could see or hear, but to go back seemed the way for cowards to move, as we did not know whether our colors were at the rear or farther to the front."

A participant described the battle in the deep woods as a "weird, uncanny contest—a battle of invisibles with invisibles." Another recounted that "men's faces were sweaty black from biting cartridges, and a sort of grim ferocity seemed to be creeping into the actions and appearance of everyone within the limited range of vision."

Warren thrust an artillery section into Saunders Field, which began lobbing shells into friend and foe. When the Federals came tumbling back, Rebels swarmed into the field and captured the guns. Warren's riflemen, however, prevented them from hauling off the pieces. "'Twas claw for claw, and the devil take us all," a Southerner recounted of the vicious hand-to-hand combat. Then the field caught fire. Wounded men tried to crawl to safety, and soldiers from both armies watched in horror as their compatriots were consumed in flames. Finally, under cover of darkness,

FISTFIGHT IN SAUNDERS FIELD

*I*n the confused swirl of combat at Saunders Field, the fighting sometimes took on a peculiarly personal tone. John Worsham of the Twenty-first Virginia Infantry described one such encounter in his book, *One of Jackson's Foot Cavalry.*

"Running midway across the little field was a gully that had been washed by the rains. In their retreat many of the enemy went into this gully for protection from our fire. When we advanced to it, we ordered them out and to the rear. All came out except one, who had hidden under an overhanging bank and was overlooked. When we fell back across the field, the Yankees who followed us to the edge of the woods shot at us as we crossed. One of our men, thinking the fire too warm, dropped into the gully for protection. Now there was a Yankee and a Confederate in the gully—and each was ignorant of the presence of the other!

After awhile they commenced to move about in the gully, there being no danger so long as they did not show themselves. Soon they came in view of each other, and they commenced to banter. Then they decided that they would go into the road and have a regular fist and skull fight, the best man to have the other as his prisoner. While both sides were firing, the two men came into the road about midway between the lines of battle, and in full view of both sides around the field. They surely created a commotion, because both sides ceased firing! When the two men took off their coats and commenced to fight with their fists, a yell went up along each line, and men rushed to the edge of the opening for a better view! The 'Johnny' soon had the 'Yank' down; the Yank surrendered, and both quietly rolled into the gully. Here they remained until nightfall, when the 'Johnny' brought the Yankee into our line. In the meantime, the disappearance of the two men into the gully was the signal for the resumption of firing. Such is war!"

A MODERN VIEW OF SAUNDERS FIELD LOOKING EAST FROM EWELL'S LINE.

(NPS)

Rebels dragged the artillery pieces into their lines.

At 2:45, Griffin strode up to Meade and Grant. He loudly announced that he had driven Ewell back three-quarters of a mile but that Sedgwick had failed to arrive and Wadsworth had been repulsed, leaving both his flanks exposed. "Who is this General Gregg? You ought to arrest him," Grant told Meade after the angry subordinate had stomped out. Meade reached over and began buttoning Grant's jacket, as though Grant were a little boy. "It's Griffin, not Gregg," Meade answered, "and it's only his way of talking."

Around 3:00 P.M., Sedgwick's lead elements reached Saunders Field. By then, fighting had sputtered to a close. A new battle erupted, however, as Sedgwick tried to overrun Ewell's line in the woods above the turnpike. Fighting seesawed as each side made fierce but inconclusive charges. Brigadier General Leroy A. Stafford, heading a Louisiana brigade, fell when a bullet severed his spine. His brigade was repulsed, as was the famed Stonewall Brigade, but the determined Louisianian waved reinforcements into battle as he lay writhing in agony. After an hour of confused and bloody combat, Sedgwick's and Ewell's warriors disengaged and began erecting earthworks. Fighting continued throughout the evening—Brigadier General John Pegram was severely wounded during an attack against his Virginia brigade—but neither side could claim advantage. Ewell had executed his assignment to perfection and stymied two Union corps.

MAY 5: HILL STOPS HANCOCK ON ORANGE PLANK ROAD

Lee's other wing under Hill started east along Orange Plank Road at sunrise, opposed by a single Federal cavalry regiment. Near noon, Hill's lead elements reached Brock Road. Meade had been alerted to Hill's approach, however, and dispatched three brigades under Brigadier General George W. Getty to defend the intersection. Getty arrived in the nick of time and, after a heated skirmish, forced Hill to retire a few hundred yards west of Brock Road. Meade was concerned that Getty could not hold for long and sent messages urging Hancock, who was waiting several miles south, to hurry to Getty's assistance with his Second Corps.

While Hill formed across Orange Plank Road in front of Getty, Lee established his headquarters a mile back at Widow Tapp's farm. He, Stuart, and Hill

were conferring when Federal infantrymen entered the clearing. The Rebel generals scrambled for safety, and the Northerners, who were equally surprised, faded into the woods, unaware that they had missed a prime opportunity to capture three top Confederate leaders. The incident dramatized the magnitude of Lee's risk. His two corps, one on the turnpike and the other on the Orange Plank Road, were dangerously divided, and the gap between them remained undefended.

Around 4:00 P.M., Meade ordered Getty to assault Hill. Hancock, whose corps was just arriving, was to pitch in as soon as possible. Getty punched through the thickets and hit Major General Henry Heth's Confederate division, which held a shallow ridge a few hundred yards west of Brock Road. Fighting tenaciously, the Rebels pinned Getty in front of their works. Hancock fed his divisions into battle as quickly as they arrived, leaving Lee

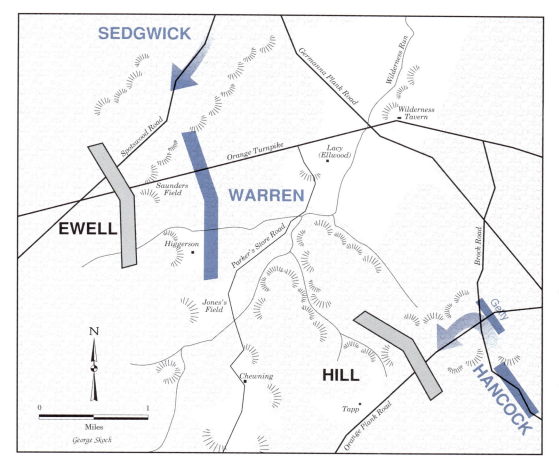

GRANT STEPS UP THE PRESSURE: MAY 5, 3:00–5:00 P.M. After repulsing Warren's initial assault, Ewell digs in at Saunders Field, while A. P. Hill, advancing up the Orange Plank Road, takes up a position just west of the Brock Road intersection, two miles to Ewell's right. At 3 P.M., Sedgwick's Sixth Corps reaches the front and engages Ewell in an indecisive action in the woods north of the turnpike. Hancock meanwhile reinforces Getty at the Brock Road intersection, and at 4:30 P.M. they attack Hill's corps on the Orange Plank Road.

no alternative but to commit his reserve division under Major General Cadmus M. Wilcox. Some of the war's most vicious fighting shook the thickets around Orange Plank Road. "A butchery pure and simple it was," a Confederate recounted, "unrelieved by any of the arts of war in which the exercise of military skill and tact robs the hour of some of its horrors. It was a mere slugging match in a dense thicket of small growth, where men but a few yards apart fired through the brushwood for hours, ceasing only when exhaustion and night commanded a rest."

Nightfall ended the combat. Hill's formation lay in shambles, and the blue and gray dug earthworks that in places stood only yards apart. A Confederate officer likened the rebel line to a rail fence that zigzagged "at every angle."

That evening, Grant planned his next move. Since Hill's corps seemed on the verge of collapsing, the Federal commander decided to concentrate his forces on Orange Plank Road. In the morning, Hancock's four divisions and Getty's three brigades were to push directly against Hill's two divisions on the roadway, while Wadsworth attacked Hill's northern flank with a force consisting of four Fifth Corps brigades. At the same time, Burnside's Ninth Corps was to advance through the interval between the turnpike and plank road, then slice south into Hill's rear. Warren and Sedgwick were to occupy Ewell on the turnpike to prevent him from reinforcing Hill. If the plan worked, Hill would be crushed and the Federals could destroy Ewell at their leisure.

Lee realized Hill's perilous situation.

"BUSHWHACKING IS THE GAME!"

While Ewell battled Warren and Sedgwick astride the Orange Turnpike, Hancock smashed into Hill's corps on the Orange Plank Road. The combat in the dark woods increased to a roar, as both sides fed additional troops into the fight. Warren L. Goss, a soldier in Hancock's

Amid the tangled, darkened woods, the 'ping! ping! ping!' the 'pop! pop! pop!' of rifles, and the long roll and roar of musketry, blending on our right and left, were terrible. In advancing it was next to impossible to preserve a distinct line, and we were constantly broken into small

times we rushed upon the enemy, but were met by a murderous fire and with heavy loss from concealed enemies. As often as we rushed forward we were compelled to get back. It was in the midst of this uproar that Mott's division gave way, and here the brave General Hayes, in endeavoring to close the break thus caused in the line, fell pierced by an enemy's bullet.

With the intention of relieving this pressure on our front, Wadsworth's division was sent from Warren's Corps southward through the woods, to fall upon Hill's rear and flank. It did not arrive in time to be of use, owing to the difficulty of making its way through the underbrush.

That night the men of this division lay on their arms, so near the enemy that during the night several parties of the rebels, while looking for water, wandered into the embraces of the enemy on the same errand.

The uproar of battle continued through the twilight hours. It was eight o'clock before the deadly crackle of musketry died gradually away, and the sad shadows of night, like a pall, fell over the dead in these ensanguined thickets. The groans and cries for water or for help from the wounded gave place to the sounds of the conflict.

With the green leaves and the darkness for their windingsheet, and the mournful whisper of the tree-tops, stirred by the breeze, for their requiem, the dead lay thick in this wild and tangled wood. This singular battle was a disconnected series of bushwhacking encounters, illustrating the tactics of savages rather than science of modern war. Thus ended the first day's fighting of the Army of the Potomac under Grant."

FOR TWO DAYS WINFIELD HANCOCK'S TROOPS GRAPPLED WITH THE CONFEDERATES ALONG THE ORANGE PLANK ROAD. IN THE END, NEITHER SIDE WAS ABLE TO GAIN AN ADVANTAGE.

(LC)

Second Corps, describes the first day's fight in the Wilderness.

"The scene of savage fighting with the ambushed enemy, which followed, defies description. No one could see the fight fifty feet from him. The roll and crackle of the musketry was something terrible, even to the veterans of many battles. The lines were very near each other, and from the dense underbrush and the tops of the trees came puffs of smoke, the 'ping!' of the bullets, and the yell of the enemy. It was a blind and bloody hunt to the death, in bewildering thickets, rather than a battle.

groups. The underbrush and briars scratched our faces, tore our clothing, and tripped our feet from under us, constantly.

On our left, a few pieces of artillery, stationed on cleared high ground, beat time to the steady roar of musketry. On the Orange Plank Road, Rickett's battery, or Kirby's, familiar to us in so many battles, was at work with its usual vigor, adding to the uproar.

"We are playing right into these devils' hands! Bushwhacking is the game! There ain't a tree in our front twenty feet high, but there is a reb up that tree!' said Wad Rider. Two, three, and four

But rather than directing Hill to rectify his formation, he decided to let the soldiers rest. Longstreet's First Corps had reached Richard's Shop, about ten miles from the battlefield, and Lee sent couriers directing Longstreet to alter his route and join Hill on the plank road. Lee expected Longstreet's fresh troops to be in place by daylight to receive Hancock's attack. The urgency for haste, however, was not adequately conveyed to Longstreet, who rested his men at Richard's Shop and did not start toward the Wilderness until after midnight. Then they lost their way cutting across fields and farm roads. As the sun rose over the Wilderness on the morning of May 6, Longstreet was nowhere to be seen.

MAY 6: LONGSTREET SAVES THE DAY

At 5:00 A.M., the Union attack rumbled up the plank road just as Grant had planned. Hill's soldiers faced an overwhelming force in front with more Federals storming in from the north. The rebel Third Corps collapsed, and gray-clad troops streamed for the rear. "It looked as if things were past mending," a Confederate admitted.

Lee had ordered Lieutenant Colonel William T. Poague's artillery to form above the plank road at Widow Tapp's farm. Poague's gunners fought valiantly to stem the blue-clad tide erupting from the far woods. Hill, who had once served in the artillery, helped work the guns. But the last-ditch effort was doomed. A few cannon, no matter how gallantly manned, could not stave off an army. It appeared that within minutes, the Army of Northern Virginia would be in shambles.

THE ARRIVAL OF JAMES LONGSTREET'S CORPS CHECKED HANCOCK'S ADVANCE AND SAVED LEE'S SUPPLY TRAINS. "LIKE A FINE LADY AT A PARTY, LONGSTREET WAS OFTEN LATE IN HIS ARRIVAL AT THE BALL," WROTE A CONFEDERATE ARTILLERIST. "BUT HE ALWAYS MADE A SENSATION AND THAT OF DELIGHT, WHEN HE GOT IN."

(LC)

Suddenly gray-clad troops pounded up the plank road from Lee's rear. "General, what brigade is this?" Lee inquired of an officer. "The Texan brigade," came the answer, which told Lee that Longstreet had arrived at last. He jerked his hat from his head and shouted, "Texans always move them!" Under the moment's excitement, Lee began advancing with the foremost troops. When the men realized that Lee was with them, they stopped and refused to budge until he went to the rear. At a staffer's urging, Lee finally consented to ride to the rear and speak with Longstreet, who by now had arrived on the field. Longstreet persuaded Lee that he had matters well in hand, and the Confederate army commander retired behind the battle front.

Longstreet's soldiers counterattacked, Major General Charles W. Field's division above the plank road and Brigadier General Joseph B. Kershaw's below. The Federals had become disordered during their advance and were in no shape to resist Longstreet's impetuous assault.

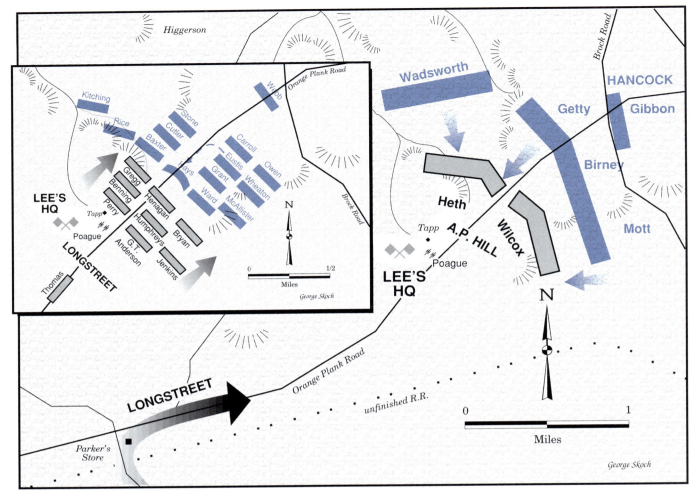

HANCOCK ROUTS HILL'S CORPS: MAY 6, 5 A.M.
At dawn, Hancock renews his attacks on Hill's corps, driving it in confusion toward the Tapp Field. Confederate artillery briefly checks Hancock's advance, and when Longstreet's corps arrives, Lee is able to push Hancock back toward the Brock Road (inset).

Within an hour, Longstreet had driven Hancock back several hundred yards east of the Tapp clearing.

The rest of Grant's well-laid scheme quickly unraveled. Burnside, whose Ninth Corps was supposed to maneuver against Hill's flank, instead fell several hours behind schedule and was finally stymied by Brigadier General Stephen D. Ramseur's Confederate brigade. Realizing that Burnside had failed in his mission, Grant ordered him to cut south through the thickets and join Hancock. Burnside's advance was so delayed that he remained unavailable to the Union war effort until after most of the important fighting had finished.

Lee remained anxious to retain the initiative. Around 10:00 A.M., his chief engineer, Major General Martin L. Smith, explored an unfinished railroad grade and discovered that it afforded access to the lower Union flank. Longstreet's aide G. Moxley Sorrel and Brigadier General William Mahone led several brigades along the unfinished grade to a point opposite Hancock's left flank. At eleven o'clock, Sorrel's men struck. As Hancock later conceded, the Rebels rolled up his line "like a wet blanket." At the same time, more of Longstreet's troops attacked along the plank road and drove Hancock just as Hill had been driven a few hours before. Wadsworth was mortally

"TEXANS ALWAYS MOVE THEM"

Among the most thrilling episodes of the Civil War occurred on May 6, 1864, in the Wilderness. At dawn, Union troops led by Major General Winfield S. Hancock attacked and routed A. P. Hill's corps on the Orange Plank Road. Lee and Hill tried desperately to rally the defeated Confederates as they came streaming back to the rear, but few men heeded their cries. Just as disaster seemed inevitable, Lieutenant General James Longstreet's First Corps arrived on the field. Longstreet's men opened ranks to let Hill's men through, then charged Hancock's men, slowly driving them back toward the Brock Road. Spearheading the attack north of the road was Brigadier General John Gregg's Texas Brigade. As the Texans moved forward, General Lee rode beside them, intent on leading the charge. His men would have none of it. In a scene that would be repeated no less than five times in the next week, the Confederates compelled Lee to go to the rear. A Texan, who identified himself only as "R. C." was witness to this dramatic event.

"The cannon thundered, musketry rolled, stragglers were fleeing, couriers riding here and there in post-haste, minnies began to sing, the dying and wounded were jolted by the flying ambulances, and filling the road-side, adding to the excitement the terror of death . . . . About this time, Gen. Lee, with his staff, rode up to Gen. Gregg—'General what brigade is this?' said Lee. 'The Texas brigade,' was General G's. reply. 'I am glad to see it,' said Lee. 'When you go in there, I wish you to give those men cold steel—they will stand and fire all day, and never move unless you charge them.' 'That is my experience,' replied the brave Gregg. By this time an aide from General Longstreet rode up and repeated the order, 'advance your command, Gen. Gregg.' And now comes the point upon which the interest of this 'o'er true tale' hangs. 'Attention Texas Brigade' was rung upon the morning air, by Gen. Gregg, 'the eyes of General Lee are upon you, forward, march." Scarce had we moved a step, when Gen. Lee, in front of the whole command, raised himself in his stirrups, uncovered his grey hairs, and with an earnest, yet anxious voice, exclaimed above the din and confusion of the hour, 'Texans always move them.' . . . A yell rent the air that must have been heard for miles around . . . . Leonard Gee, a courier to Gen. Gregg, and riding by my side, with tears coursing down his cheeks and yells issuing from his throat exclaimed, 'I would charge hell itself for that old man.' It was not what Gen. Lee said that so infused and excited the men, as his tone and look, which each one of us knew were born of the dangers of the hour.

With yell after yell we moved forward, passed the brow of the hill, and moved down the declivity towards the undergrowth—a distance in all not exceeding 200 yards. After moving over half the ground we all saw that Gen. Lee was following us into battle—care and anxiety upon his countenance—refusing to come back at the request and advice of his staff. If I recollect correctly, the brigade halted when they discovered Gen. Lee's intention, and all eyes were turned upon him. Five and six of his staff would gather around him, seize him, his arms, his horse's reins, but he shook them off and

moved forward. Thus did he continue until just before we reached the undergrowth, not, however, until the balls began to fill and whistle through the air. Seeing that we would do all that men could do to retrieve the misfortunes of the hour, accepting the advice of his staff, and hearkening to the protest of his advancing soldiers, he at last turned round and rode back."

AT WILDERNESS AND AGAIN AT SPOTSYLVANIA LEE ATTEMPTED TO LEAD HIS TROOPS INTO BATTLE. EACH TIME, HIS SOLDIERS SHOUTED HIM BACK.

(NPS)

wounded, and Hancock's wing retired to Brock Road.

As his Rebels began clearing the plank road of the enemy, a triumphant Longstreet rode forward with several officers. Some of Mahone's Virginians involved in the flank attack had meanwhile crossed the plank road and were returning. They spied the headquarters cavalcade, mistook it for Federals, and opened fire. Longstreet fell with a severe wound through his neck, and one of his most promising brigade commanders, Brigadier General Micah Jenkins, was killed. Commentators later

LEE TO THE REAR!
CRIED THE TEXANS.
MAY 6, 1864.

caught fire but lacked the manpower to exploit the breakthrough. His failed attack against Hancock's Brock Road line represented the last major offensive attempted by the Army of Northern Virginia.

MAY 6: GORDON ATTACKS SEDGWICK'S FLANK

Early in the morning, Brigadier General John B. Gordon scouted the northern Union flank and discovered that it was unprotected. He recommended to Ewell that the Confederates attack this vulnerable point, but Gordon's immediate superior, Major General Jubal A. Early, thought the venture too risky. Gordon, however, continued to urge a flank attack, and toward evening, Ewell relented. According to Gordon's version, Lee visited Ewell's sector and ordered the corps commander to execute Gordon's plan. Other sources cast doubt on whether Lee intervened as Gordon claimed.

Shortly before dark, Ewell authorized Gordon to launch the attack that he had been urging. Sedgwick's line crumpled, and confusion at Union headquarters was extreme. An aide ran to Grant with advice. "General Grant, this is a crisis that cannot be looked upon too seriously," he warned. "I know Lee's methods well by past experience; he will throw his own army between us and the Rapidan, and cut us off completely from our communications." Grant exploded. "Oh, I am heartily tired of hearing about what Lee is going to do," he roared back. "Some of you seem to think he is suddenly going to turn a double somersault, and land in our rear and on both of our flanks at the same time. Go back to your command, and try to think what we are going to do ourselves, instead

reflected on parallels between Longstreet's wounding and the shooting of Thomas J. "Stonewall" Jackson. The two prominent Confederate generals had been shot by their own men while executing successful flanking maneuvers, and the incidents had occurred almost a year apart and in the Wilderness. As one of Lee's aides later remarked, "the old deacon would say that God willed it thus."

Longstreet's wounding, along with disorienting wooded terrain, stalled the attack that Longstreet had so skillfully initiated. Lee labored to resume the offensive but was unable to position his troops until after four o'clock. By then, Hancock had ensconced his corps behind imposing earthworks lining Brock Road. Lee assaulted and gained an advantage when the works

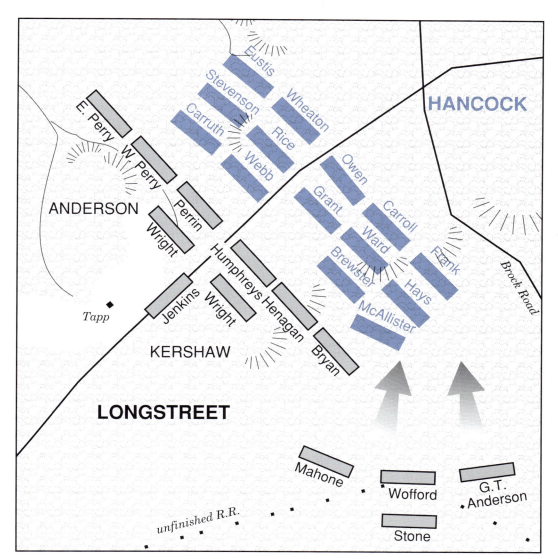

of what Lee is going to do."

Darkness descended before Gordon could consolidate his gains, and Union reinforcements prevented him from reaching the Federal rear. Sedgwick established a new line during the night, its upper flank thrown back across Germanna Plank Road. For years afterward, Gordon rankled at what he viewed as a lost opportunity. While his superiors waited, he claimed, "the greatest opportunity ever presented to Lee's army was permitted to pass. Critics would later quibble over whether Gordon had exaggerated his

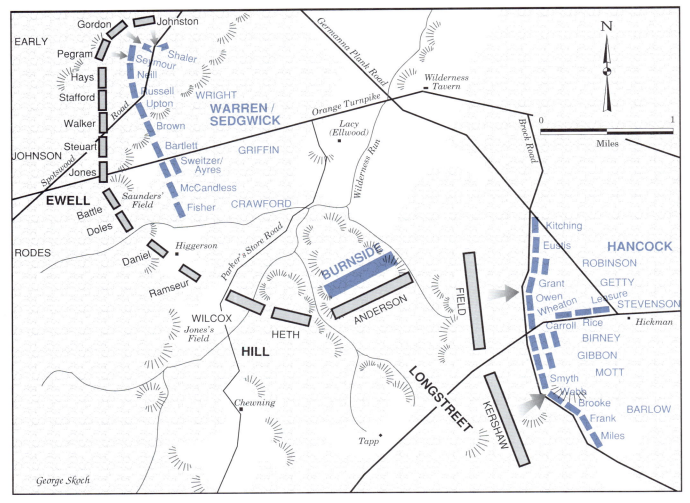

FINAL ATTACKS: 2 P.M. TO DARK, MAY 6

Burnside's corps launches a feeble attack on Anderson's division in the woods north of the plank road, while Lee marshals Longstreet's corps for a massive, but unsuccessful, attack on Hancock's Brock Road defenses. To the north, Ewell holds Warren in place near the Orange Turnpike and at dusk attacks Sedgwick's exposed right flank, scattering the brigades of Shaler and Seymour.

attack's potential, but none could deny that delaying the assault had cost Lee dearly.

MAY 7: GRANT TO LEAVE THE WILDERNESS

On the morning of May 7, Grant and Lee faced each other across a smoldering wasteland. Neither general could claim victory. Lee had fought Grant to an impasse but had failed to drive him away. And Grant had failed in his objective of destroying Lee. "There lay both armies," a Union aide wrote home, "each behind its breastworks, panting and exhausted, and scowling at each other."

Lee held a strong position along high ground. Rather than attacking Lee's formidable earthworks, Grant decided to rely on maneuver. By dropping south on Brock Road to Spotsylvania, he hoped to interpose between Lee and Richmond, leaving Lee no choice but to abandon the Wilderness and fight on ground of Grant's choosing. His goal for the first day's march was the crossroads hamlet of Spotsylvania Court House, some ten miles south on Brock Road.

At 6:30 A.M., Grant ordered Meade to make "all preparations for a night march" to Spotsylvania. The army was to move south by two routes. Hancock's Second Corps would remain in place while Warren's Fifth Corps slid behind it and continued down Brock Road to Spotsylvania. Once Warren had passed, Hancock would follow. At the same time, Sedgwick was to start along Orange Plank Road toward Chancellorsville, followed by Burnside's Ninth Corps. By morning on the eighth, Grant expected his army to mass near the court house hamlet.

Meade began by ordering Major General Philip Sheridan's cavalry to clear the way. Thus far, the Federal mounted arm had performed poorly. On May 5, Wilson's division had been isolated on Catharpin Road by Brigadier General Thomas L. Rosser's Rebels and had fought a bitter action before escaping. On the sixth, Brigadier General George A. Custer had inflicted serious casualties on Rosser north of Todd's Tavern, but Sheridan had been compelled to withdraw to protect the army's supply wagons. Thus, on the morning of May 7, Sheridan's mission was to recapture the ground that he had forfeited on the sixth and to clear Brock Road to Spotsylvania.

Sheridan started south but was blocked above Todd's Tavern by Virginia cavalrymen under Major General Fitzhugh Lee. During early afternoon, Sheridan was able to bring most of his corps into play and drove Lee from the tavern. A cavalry

GRANT PUSHES SOUTH

For the Union army, the Battle of the Wilderness had been a decided failure. Two days of fighting in the tangled thickets had resulted in some 18,000 Union casualties, almost as many as Hooker had sustained at Chancellorsville and considerably more than Burnside had suffered at Fredericksburg. Lee, by contrast, probably suffered fewer than 12,000 casualties. Both Burnside and Hooker had retreated across the Rappahannock following their battles with Lee, but Grant did not. In one of the most far-reaching decisions of the war, he directed his engineers to take up the pontoon bridges at Germanna Ford on May 7 and issued orders to his corps commanders to march toward

accompanied by their staffs, after having given personal supervision to the starting of the march, rode along the Brock road toward Hancock's headquarters, with the intention of waiting there till Warren's troops should reach that point. While moving close to Hancock's line, there occurred an unexpected demonstration on the part of the troops, which created one of the most memorable scenes of the campaign. Notwithstanding the darkness of the night, the form of the commander was recognized, and word was passed rapidly along that the chief who had led them through the mazes of the Wilderness was again moving forward with his horse's head turned toward Richmond.

echoed through the forest, and glad shouts of triumph rent the air. Men swung their hats, tossed up their arms, and pressed forward to within touch of their chief, clapping their hands, and speaking to him with the familiarity of comrades. Pine-knots and leaves were set on fire, and lighted the scene with their weird, flickering glare. The night march had become a triumphal procession for the new commander. The demonstration was the emphatic verdict pronounced by the troops upon his first battle in the East. The excitement had been imparted to the horses, which soon became restive, and even the general's large bay, over which he possessed ordinarily such perfect control,

UNION TROOPS
CHEERED GRANT
ON THE MARCH TO
SPOTSYLVANIA
COURT HOUSE.

(LC)

manders to march toward Spotsylvania Court House that night. When Union soldiers discovered that Grant was pushing ahead despite his losses, they cheered him. They had finally found a general who would continue to fight Lee until he beat him. In the following excerpt, Grant's aide-de-camp, Colonel Horace Porter, describes this unexpected ovation that took place in the depths of the Wilderness.

"Soon after dark, Generals Grant and Meade,

turned toward Richmond. Troops know but little about what is going on in a large army, except the occurrences which take place in their immediate vicinity; but this night ride of the general-in-chief told plainly the story of success, and gave each man to understand that the cry was to be 'On to Richmond!' Soldiers weary and sleepy after their long battle, with stiffened limbs and smarting wounds, now sprang to their feet, forgetful of their pains, and rushed forward to the roadside. Wild cheers

became difficult to manage. Instead of being elated by this significant ovation, the general, thoughtful only of the practical question of the success of the movement, said: 'This is most unfortunate. The sound will reach the ears of the enemy, and I fear it may reveal our movement.' By his direction, staff-officers rode forward and urged the men to keep quiet so as not to attract the enemy's attention; but the demonstration did not really cease until the general was out of sight."

battle took shape on two fronts. Colonel J. Irvin Gregg's Federal horsemen elbowed west on Catharpin Road but were stopped at Corbin's Bridge by Rebel horsemen under Major Generals Wade Hampton and William H. F. "Rooney" Lee. Gregg retired to a field west of Todd's Tavern, formed his brigade behind makeshift earthworks of logs and fence rails, and repelled a series of Confederate assaults. For the rest of the day, Hampton and Rooney Lee waged a bitter but inconclusive fight against Gregg on Catharpin Road.

Brigadier General Wesley Merritt meanwhile continued south in pursuit of Fitzhugh Lee. He met his quarry about a mile below Todd's Tavern, where Lee's

men had dismounted and formed behind makeshift barricades. From about 4:00 P.M. until dark, Merritt and Lee fought one of the war's bloodiest cavalry engagements. Federal horsemen charged down the road-way only to be shot from their horses. Then Lee's barricades caught fire, which forced the Rebels to retire to a second line of works. More Federals reinforced Merritt, and it looked as though Lee would be defeated. Night, however, intervened, and Sheridan decided against continuing to fight in darkness. In a move reminiscent of his actions on the sixth, he abandoned much of the road that he had opened and ordered his troopers to bivouac at Todd's Tavern. A Confederate cavalryman echoed

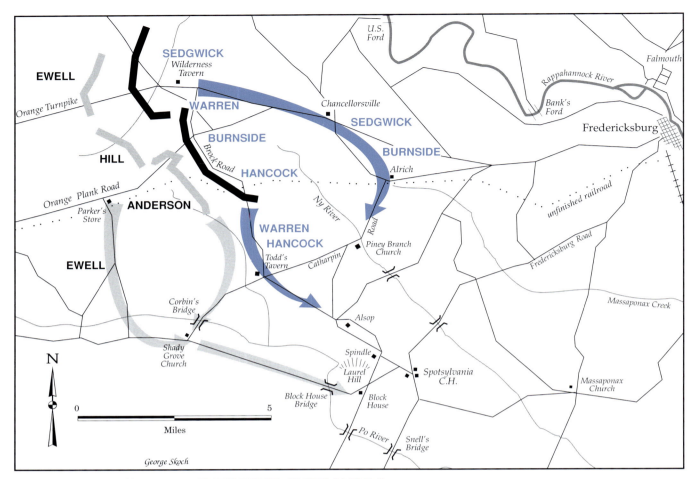

THE RACE TO SPOTSYLVANIA COURT HOUSE: NIGHT, MAY 7–8

Stymied in the Wilderness, Grant orders Meade to march to Spotsylvania Court House. Warren's Fifth Corps leads the march down the Brock Road, followed by Hancock, while Burnside and Sedgwick swing farther east. Anticipating Grant's move, Lee likewise orders his army to Spotsylvania. Anderson's corps follows a military road to the Catharpin Road, then follows the Shady Grove Church Road to Spotsylvania. Ewell's corps follows Anderson to Spotsylvania, marching by way of Parker's Store, leaving Hill to hold the Wilderness line.

a common sentiment as he contemplated the corpse-strewn road. "What a curse war is," he scrawled in his diary. "The dreadful sights I have seen this week in the Wilderness will never be banished from my memories."

Around 8:00 P.M., Grant's infantrymen began pursuing their assigned routes south. They proceeded at a snail's pace. Slow wagons and ambulances blocked the way, traffic jams occurred at unexpected places, and exhausted foot soldiers slogged along without enthusiasm. Meade's provost marshal termed the episode "one of the most fatiguing and disgraceful rides I ever took." Meade, who rode at the army's head, did not reach Todd's Tavern until

after midnight and was infuriated to find Sheridan's cavalry camped there. The army ground to a halt as Meade dispatched the horsemen to try again to clear the way south.

Lee had been trying to fathom Grant's intentions and concluded that Grant meant either to retire to Fredericksburg or push south. In either event, Spotsylvania loomed importantly, so Lee directed his artillery chief Brigadier General William N. Pendleton to cut a road through the woods from the lower Confederate flank to Catharpin Road. Toward the end of the day, Lee instructed Longstreet's replacement—General Richard H. Anderson—to start south along

the makeshift road. Lee did not perceive
the need for haste, but smoke from the
burning woods and stench from unburied
bodies induced Anderson to start early. He
was under way around ten o'clock and followed the woods path to Catharpin Road.
There he turned west, crossed the Po, then
cut southeast on Shady Grove Church
Road toward Spotsylvania.

Lee and Grant were in a race to
Spotsylvania. The fate of the campaign
would turn on who got there first.

MAY 8: GRANT AND LEE MEET AT LAUREL HILL

Fitzhugh Lee's cavalrymen used the
night of May 7–8 to strengthen their log
barricades across Brock Road. At morning's
first light, Brigadier General Wesley
Merritt's Union cavalry division attacked
the makeshift blockades with little success.
Warren's Fifth Corps meanwhile advanced
to the front. Around 7:00 A.M., when it
became clear that Merritt was stymied,
Meade ordered Warren to punch through
with infantry.

The Union Fifth Corps started down
Brock Road, Brigadier General John C.
Robinson's division leading, followed by
Griffin's. Fitzhugh Lee's exhausted horse-

men retired before superior numbers.
About a mile south, at the Alsop place,
Brock Road split into two branches that
bowed apart, then joined again on the
Spindle farm's northern edge. James
Breathed, who was commanding Fitzhugh
Lee's horse artillery, made a stirring stand
at the Alsop place until one of his guns
became mired in the freshly plowed field.
"Surrender that gun, you rebel scoundrel!"
Northerners hollered as they approached
the piece. Breathed freed the gun from its
injured team, mounted the wheel horse,
and brought the piece to safety through a
hail of bullets, all the while brazenly
thumbing his nose at the Yankees.

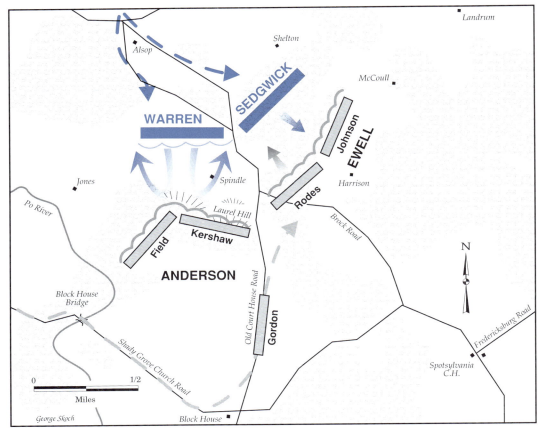
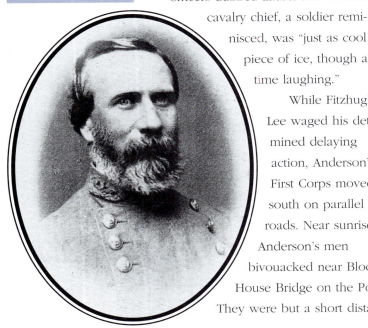

In a final attempt to stem the blue-clad tide cresting down Brock Road, Fitzhugh Lee formed his division along a shallow ridge below the Spindle clearing. Jeb Stuart arrived and helped Lee stake out his formation along the rise, which Union officers dubbed Laurel Hill. The Rebel cavalry chief, a soldier reminisced, was "just as cool as a piece of ice, though all the time laughing."

While Fitzhugh Lee waged his determined delaying action, Anderson's First Corps moved south on parallel roads. Near sunrise, Anderson's men bivouacked near Block House Bridge on the Po. They were but a short distance

from Laurel Hill and breakfasted to the rattle of musketry from Lee's and Warren's bitter action. Suddenly messengers from Lee pounded up with pleas for Anderson's help. He hurried his foremost units—the brigades of Colonel John W. Henagan and of Brigadier General Benjamin G. Humphreys, along with Major John C. Haskell's artillery battalion—toward Laurel Hill. As Anderson's men reached the back side of the ridge, Stuart waved them into place. According to witnesses, Warren's Federals were no more than a hundred yards away. Lee had been saved by a last-minute rescue that modern Hollywood could scarcely rival.

Warren assumed that only cavalry occupied the far ridge and ordered his troops ahead. "Never mind cannon! Never mind bullets! Press on and clear this road," he reportedly shouted, then added in a more practical vein: "It's the only way to get to your rations."

The Union charge dissolved into a rout. Troops advancing east of Brock Road dropped into a depression and found themselves pinned against the steep side of Laurel Hill by Confederate musketry whizzing overhead. Units west of the road-

managed and their numerical advantage "dissipated by dribbling into the attack regiment after regiment, each succeeding one too late to be of any service to the one that had gone before." Another mumbled, "There appeared to have been a miscalculation somewhere."

AS HIS TROOPS CAME TUMBLING BACK IN CON- FUSION FROM LAUREL HILL, GOUVERNEUR WARREN RALLIED THEM AROUND THE FLAG OF THE THIRTEENTH MASSACHUSETTS VOLUNTEERS.

(LC)

way were slammed by blistering fire as they reached a high spot in the field near the Spindle house. Some of Griffin's soldiers managed to reach the Confederate works but lacked the support necessary to achieve a breakthrough. As his remaining divisions arrived—Crawford's Pennsylvania Reserves and Cutler's division, formerly under Wadsworth—Warren pushed them into the melee. The result was tremendous Union casualties.

By noon, Warren had abandoned any pretext of taking Laurel Hill by storm and began concentrating instead on massing his corps behind earthworks along the Spindle clearing's northern edge. Soldiers complained that the affair had been poorly

MAY 8: WILSON OCCUPIES SPOTSYLVANIA COURTHOUSE

While Warren sparred south along Brock Road, Wilson's Union cavalry division trotted toward Spotsylvania Court House on an easterly route along the Fredericksburg Road. Wilson's troopers entered the hamlet around 8:00 A.M. and found it unprotected. The young cavalry commander recognized that he was superbly located. By sweeping north on Brock Road, he could take the Confederates on Laurel Hill in the rear.

Wilson dispatched a brigade under Colonel John B. McIntosh up Brock Road.

HOT-TEMPERED PHIL SHERIDAN CHAFED FOR AN OPPORTUNITY TO FIGHT JEB STUART'S CONFEDERATE CAVALRY IN A PITCHED BATTLE. HE WOULD SOON GET HIS CHANCE.

(LC)

Stuart had a single regiment to spare, which bravely but unsuccessfully attempted to detain McIntosh. Meanwhile, Anderson learned of Wilson's threat and dispatched infantry above and below Spotsylvania Court House to catch the Union cavalry division. At the last moment, a courier arrived from Sheridan and directed Wilson to withdraw. With Rebels lashing his rear guard, Wilson retired up the Fredericksburg Road as he had come.

Wilson's near capture brought Meade's and Sheridan's simmering feud to a boil. In Meade's opinion, Sheridan had thoroughly botched his assignment to clear the road to Spotsylvania. As Sheridan saw it, Meade had meddled in his management of the cavalry and had nearly gotten Wilson captured. Sheridan stormed over to Meade's tent in a hot rage. According to an aide who witnessed the encounter, Meade

had "worked himself into a towering passion regarding the delays encountered in the forward movement." Another witness described Sheridan's language as "highly spiced and conspicuously italicized with expletives." The confrontation ended with Sheridan proclaiming that he could whip Stuart if Meade would only let him, then stomping out of the tent.

Meade walked to Grant's tent and repeated the conversation, including Sheridan's remarks about beating Stuart if Meade would only let him. "Well, he generally knows what he is talking about," Grant answered, and added: "Let him start right out and do it."

At 1:00 P.M., Sheridan received orders directing him to concentrate his command and "proceed against the enemy's cavalry." During the rest of the afternoon, he gathered his units at Alrich's and provisioned them for an early march.

MAY 8: HANCOCK DEFENDS TODD'S TAVERN

During the morning of May 8, Hancock's Federal Second Corps formed across Catharpin Road immediately west of Todd's Tavern to guard against a Confederate attack from the rear. Late in the afternoon, the Rebel Third Corps approached Hancock's pickets on Catharpin Road. Hill, who suffered from a recurrent malady, had become too sick to command and had been temporarily replaced by Major General Jubal A. Early, one of Lee's more flamboyant lieutenants. Early decided to probe toward Todd's Tavern and gave the assignment to Mahone.

Mahone's division, assisted by Confederate cavalry, encountered Brigadier

General Francis C. Barlow's division, which had thrust west along Catharpin Road. A vicious fight flared along the roadway as Barlow retired to entrenchments near Todd's Tavern. Early, however, decided against pressing the matter and withdrew west to Shady Grove Church, where he camped for the night. "And so the Second Corps stood to arms," one of Hancock's aides wrote, "all the afternoon and into the early evening, believing that another of its great days of battle had come." But the expected onslaught never arrived. As the aide later put it, "darkness came on, and the great battle of Todd's Tavern was never fought."

MAY 8: MEADE AGAIN ATTACKS LAUREL HILL

During the afternoon, Sedgwick's Sixth Corps tramped past Alsop's and extended Warren's line eastward. It was unseasonably hot and dusty and nothing seemed to be going right. One of Sedgwick's aides later explained that his "dim impression of that afternoon is of things going wrong, of much bloodshed and futility." Meade's staffer Theodore Lyman thought that "never were officers and men more jaded and prostrated."

By seven o'clock in the evening, Meade had managed to coordinate

WILLIAM MAHONE TOOK COMMAND OF ANDERSON'S DIVISION ON MAY 7 AND LED IT THROUGHOUT THE BATTLE OF SPOTSYLVANIA.

(LC)

Sedgwick and Warren. Several New Jersey regiments punched forward near Brock Road only to be shredded by Anderson's firepower. Survivors sought refuge in dips and swales. Many waited until darkness before attempting to crawl to safety. East of the roadway, Crawford's Pennsylvanians and several Sixth Corps units charged ahead in hopes of slipping past Anderson's right flank. They received a nasty surprise. Ewell's Confederate Second Corps had left the Wilderness early that morning and arrived in time to shift next to Anderson. The Federals were repulsed and pursued to their works by Battle's Alabamians.

Musketry sparked through the night as snipers fought nasty little battles in the no-man's land between the armies. Disappointment in the Union ranks was palpable. "The thing was so poorly executed that it does not amount to much," a Northerner wrote home.

Meade complained to his aide Lyman as they sat around the evening campfire. Sedgwick, he grumbled, was "constitutionally slow," but his real anger was directed at Warren. "I told Warren today that he lost his nerve," Meade explained, "at which he professed to be very indignant." Following a rancorous meeting with his corps commanders, Meade ordered them to rectify their lines and rest their men. Grant's offensive was assuming a decidedly defensive cast.

MAY 9: A SHARP-SHOOTER KILLS SEDGWICK

The sun rose on May 9 to reveal a network of earthen fortifications sprawling above Spotsylvania Court House. The Confederate line started near the Po, followed Laurel Hill east across Brock Road, then lunged forward to form a horseshoe-

shaped bulge encompassing high ground around the Harrison and McCoull places. Federal entrenchments wound through fields and woods across from the Rebels. A Union reporter thought that "it was Gettysburg reversed—Lee having the inner circle." The salient—or "Muleshoe," as the projecting earthworks were called—concerned Lee's engineers because it constituted a vulnerable point in the Rebel position. They deemed it a "necessary evil," however, as it was important to include high ground within the salient.

Andrew A. Humphreys, remarked that "with such entrenchments as these, having artillery throughout, with flank fire along their lines wherever practicable, and with the rifled muskets then in use, which were as effective at three hundred yards as the smooth-bore muskets at sixty yards, the strength of an army sustaining attack was more than quadrupled."

A Confederate in the Stonewall Brigade wrote home: "Wonder what General Grant thinks of Master Bob today, for he is right in his way to Richmond."

Ewell's Confederate Second Corps occupied the Muleshoe. The Southerners dug trenches with cups and bayonets, felled trees in front to create clear fields of fire, then stacked the timber with sharpened branches facing the enemy, intending to delay the Yankees while they shot them to pieces. Earthworks were erected in front of the trenches and head logs were thrown on top with "loopholes" for firing. Every so often barricades—called "traverses"—extended back at right angles from the main works to protect the Rebels from flanking fire and to give them rallying points if the Federals broke through. Meade's chief of staff, Major General

Around nine o'clock in the morning, Sedgwick inspected his dispositions near Brock Road. Rebel sharpshooters were active and had already shot Brigadier General William H. Morris in the leg. Bullets spattered around and men began ducking. "What! What! Men dodging this way for single bullets," Sedgwick exclaimed. "What will you do when they open fire along the whole line. I am ashamed of you. They couldn't hit an elephant at this distance." Just then a sergeant dropped to his knees, and Sedgwick prodded the man with his boot. "What are you dodging at?" Sedgwick inquired. "They can't hit an elephant at that distance." The sergeant explained that he believed in dodging and thought that the practice had once saved his life. "All right, my man," Sedgwick laughed. "Go to your place." There was another shrill whistle and a dull thump. Blood spurt like a little fountain from under Sedgwick's left eye, and the fatally wounded general collapsed into an aide's arms.

Sedgwick's death was sorely felt. "From the commander to the lowest private, he had no enemy," an aide scrawled to his family. Meade appointed Major General Horatio G. Wright as the Sixth Corps' new head.

The day's chief activities occurred on the flanks. Burnside's corps, which was quartered near Alrich's, began south along the Fredericksburg Road. Brigadier General Orlando B. Willcox's division reached the Gayle house above the Ni, threw skirmishers over the creek, then advanced partway up the far bank to the Beverly house. There they met determined resistance from Fitzhugh Lee's mounted Confederates.

Fighting sputtered back and forth until about noon, when Brigadier General Thomas G. Stevenson's division pulled up and joined Willcox. Burnside was concerned, however, that his corps projected dangerously in front of Meade and directed Willcox and Stevenson to entrench.

From his observation post at the Gayle house, Willcox could see church spires near Spotsylvania Court House. He was distressed to see Confederates there and expressed concern that they might attack. Meanwhile, Hancock, who was still near Todd's Tavern, reported that Early had left his sector. Grant concluded from Willcox's and Hancock's intelligence that Lee must be shifting from west to east, possibly to thrust toward Fredericksburg. Sheridan had left on his raid toward Richmond, so Grant was without his mounted arm to gather information. Nonetheless, based on the reports from his flanks, he decided to exploit Lee's apparent maneuver and launch an offensive of his own. Burnside was to hold the Ni while Hancock advanced to the Po and attacked Lee's western flank. Burnside would be the anvil and Hancock the hammer while the rest of the Union army— Warren and Wright—watched for an opening to attack across Lee's entire line.

Grant visited Hancock late in the afternoon. Union artillery opened on Confederate wagons across the Po, and soon Hancock's infantry was splashing across. By dark, most of the Federal Second Corps was over the river and massing near Block House Bridge, near the left end of Lee's line. The river bent sharply south at the bridge, which meant that Hancock would have to cross the Po a second time to reach the enemy. Fearing that Lee had the bridge heavily guarded, Hancock

deferred advancing until the next morning. Pontoons were thrown across the Po at the initial crossing to expedite Hancock's retreat, should it become necessary.

Hancock's delay cost Grant dearly. Under cover of darkness, Lee withdrew two divisions of Early's corps from Spotsylvania Court House and rushed them toward the endangered Po River sector. Mahone formed across the Confederate flank while Heth circled below Hancock, then swung north to strike the Federal Second Corps' flank. In a move characteristic of his military style, Lee was turning the tables on Grant.

MAY 10: HETH ATTACKS HANCOCK BELOW THE PO

On the morning of May 10, Hancock's corps lay stretched along Shady Grove Church Road from Block House

Bridge to Waite's Shop. The situation was hardly encouraging. Mahone held the far bank and Heth was approaching from below. Hancock's expedition was running into serious trouble.

By 10:00 A.M., Grant realized that he had misapprehended Lee's dispositions. The Confederates were not shifting east as he had thought. It was apparent, however, that Lee had shifted troops to attack Hancock, and Grant's best guess was that they had come from Laurel Hill. Acting on that assumption, Grant formulated a new plan. Hancock was to withdraw from the Po and leave a single division behind to distract Lee. The rest of the army was to attack across Lee's formation at 5:00 P.M. As Grant saw it, a coordinated assault was bound to find Lee's weak point.

Hancock withdrew from the Po and began forming on Warren's right flank. A single Union division—Barlow's—remained below the Po to mislead Lee into believing that Grant still meant to attack there. Around two in the afternoon, Heth's lead elements broke into the fields around Waite's Shop. Jubal Early had come along and was in a fighting mood. While Barlow's men hunkered behind makeshift entrenchments along Shady Grove Church Road, Heth's men shifted into a battle line and charged with high-pitched screams. "The combat now became close and bloody," Hancock observed. "The rebs came up yelling as if they'd got a special license to thresh us," a Federal soldier recounted.

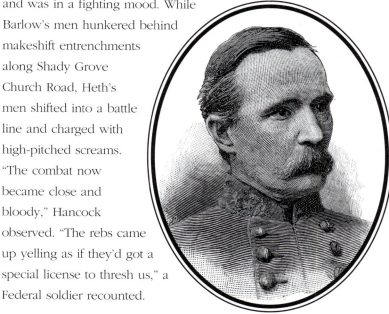

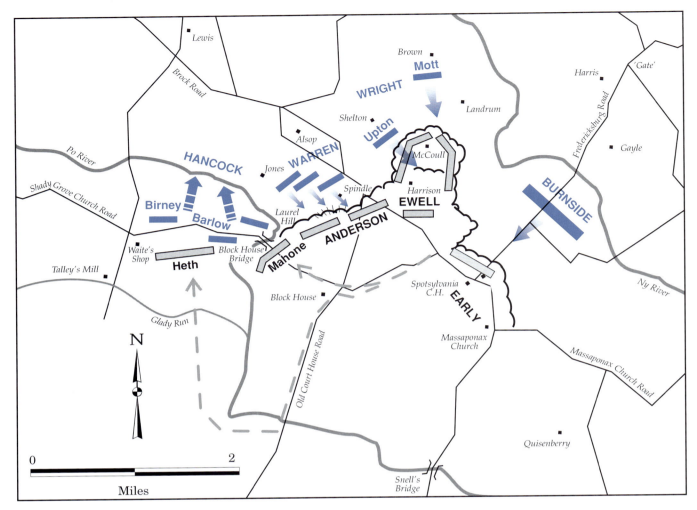

GRANT SEEKS AN OPENING: MAY 10
Lee sends Heth's and Mahone's divisions of Early's corps to attack Hancock, south of the Po River, leaving Early with just one division to hold Spotsylvania Court House against Burnside's Ninth Corps. Warren continues his fruitless assaults at Laurel Hill, at the cost of hundreds of Union lives, while Upton and Mott attack Ewell's position at the Muleshoe Salient.

Barlow resisted bravely but found himself in an impossible situation as Rebel artillery from across the Po lobbed shells into his men and the surrounding woods caught fire. "Many of the gallant wounded perished in the flames," Hancock explained. Step by step, Barlow's survivors funneled through a mile-long clearing back to the Po. It was a deadly gauntlet—"flames were crackling and roaring," a soldier recounted, and shells exploded all around—but most of the division managed to escape. The last troops—soldiers from Brigadier General Nelson A. Miles's brigade—scurried over the remaining pontoon bridge. Union engineers cut the ropes holding the span and watched it drift to the Po's northern bank.

The Battle of the Po, as Barlow's and Heth's fight came to be called, was a bloody little affair. Early congratulated Heth and later claimed that the operation "relieved us from a very threatening danger, as the position the enemy had attained would have enabled him to completely enfilade [Anderson's] position and get possession of the line of our communications to the rear." Hancock congratulated Barlow for extricating his soldiers from a difficult situation. "Not a regiment gave way for a moment in the critical movement," he wrote.

"The Confederates did not hasten the pace by anything they did; our troops retired just when and as they were directed."

Grant's handling of the Po operation was severely criticized. By starting the maneuver late in the day, he denied Hancock opportunity to complete the ruse before the Confederates had time to respond. A rebel artillery commander later remarked that "it was a great, an immense piece of luck for us that Hancock had made his move across the Po late in the afternoon, giving us the night to make preparations to meet him."

MAY 10: GRANT ASSAULTS LEE'S LINE

Grant planned a massive assault at five o'clock in the afternoon across Lee's entire line in hopes of overwhelming the Confederates. The scheme began to unravel around 2:00 P.M., when Hancock returned to the Po to help extricate Barlow. Hancock's departure left Warren in charge of the Laurel Hill sector. The Fifth Corps commander was still smarting from

earlier reverses and was anxious to redeem his reputation. As soon as Hancock left, he petitioned Meade for permission to attack Laurel Hill right away, unsupported and before the scheduled five o'clock advance. For reasons that have never been explained, Meade consented to Warren's request.

At about 4:00 P.M., Warren led elements from the Second and Fifth Corps against Laurel Hill. A witness summarized the results. "Some portions of the corps advanced to the abatis, others halted part way and discharged a few volleys, but speedily the whole line fell back with terrible loss." A few units elbowed through smoldering cedars only to become mired in a freshly plowed field. "How we got through it all I don't know," a Union survivor reminisced.

Grant had no choice but to postpone the grand assault until Warren

WAITING TO ATTACK

*I*n his efforts to find a weak spot in Lee's defenses, Grant ordered a series of attacks against the Confederate line on May 10. By far the most successful of these ventures was an attack led by Colonel Emory Upton of the Sixth Corps. Just before sundown, Upton led 5,000 men in a charge against the western face of the Muleshoe salient, overrunning the Confederate line them in, but they were firing from their breastworks, on top of which they had logs to protect their heads. Our batteries (one on the right and three in the rear of us) were belching away at them, and they were answering but feebly. Occasionally the hum of a bullet and the screech of a shell gave notice that they were on the *qui vive*.

As soon as we were been bright and it-was warm, but the air felt damp, indicating rain. The racket and smoke made by the skirmishers and batteries, made it look hazy about us, and we had to raise our voices to be heard. We waited in suspense for some time. Dorr Davenport, with whom I tented, said to me, 'I feel as though I was going to get hit. If I do, you get my things and send them home.' I

and taking some 1,000 prisoners. The 121st New York Volunteers, a regiment Upton had commanded earlier in the war, was in the first line of battle. Clinton Beckwith, an officer in the regiment, described the tension in the ranks as the time of attack approached.

"About 5 P.M. we moved over the works down into the woods, close up to our skirmishers (the 65th N.Y.), who were keeping up a rapid fire, and formed in line of battle. Regiment after regiment came up and formed in line, we being in the first or front line and the right of the column . . . . The Rebel rifle pits were about two hundred and fifty yards in front of our skirmish line. They had no skirmishers out, ours having driven

formed Colonel Upton, Major Galpin and the Adjutant came along and showed to the officers and men a sketch of just how the Rebel works were located, and we were directed to keep to the right of the road which ran from our line direct to theirs . . . . We were ordered to fix bayonets, to load and cap our guns and to charge at a right shoulder shift arms. No man was to stop and succor or assist a wounded comrade. We must go as far as possible, and when we broke their line, face to our right, advance and fire lengthwise of their line. Colonel Upton was with our regiment and rode on our right. He instructed us not to fire a shot, cheer or yell, until we struck the works. It was nearly sundown when we were ready to go forward. The day had

said, 'I will, and you do the same for me in case I am shot, but keep a stiff upper lip. We may get through all right.' He said, 'I dread the first volley, they have so good a shot at us.' Shortly after this the batteries stopped firing, and in a few minutes an officer rode along toward the right as fast as he could, and a moment afterward word was passed along to get ready, then 'Fall in,' and then 'Forward.' I felt my gorge rise, and my stomach and intestines shrink together in a knot, and a thousand things rushed through my mind. I fully realized the terrible peril I was to encounter. I looked about in the faces of the boys around me, and they told the tale of expected death. Pulling my cap down over my eyes, I stepped out. . . ."

RESPONSIBILITY FOR THE SIXTH CORPS' MAY 10 ATTACK ON THE MULESHOE FELL TO TWENTY-FOUR-YEAR-OLD EMORY UPTON.

(LC)

could reconstitute his formation. Word of the delay, however, apparently never reached Brigadier General Gershom Mott, and at 5:00 P.M. he charged alone toward the tip of the Confederate salient. "On reaching the open field," one of his officers reported, "the enemy opened his batteries, enfilading our lines and causing our men to fall back in confusion."

Sometime after six o'clock, the Sixth Corps launched its phase of the attack, led by Colonel Emory Upton and a select force of twelve regiments. Upton quietly assembled his troops at the edge of the woods across from the salient's western leg and instructed them to charge without pausing to fire or load. His front line was to breach the works and then spread right and left along the Rebel trenches, widening the cleft, and his remaining units were to consolidate the gains.

Union artillery pounded the Rebel works in front of Upton, then fell silent.

"Forward!" sounded the command. "I felt my gorge rise, and my stomach and intestines shrink together in a knot, and a thousand things rushed through my mind," a Northerner recounted. Upton's blue-clad host swept across the field. A volley spewed from the Rebel works, then another. Gaps appeared in Upton's formation, but the men kept on, clawing through the abatis and over the entrenchments.

At first, the plan went like clockwork. After rupturing the works, Upton's Federals splayed along the trenches in each direction, virtually annihilating Brigadier General George P. Doles's Georgians. Lee and Ewell feverishly organized a counterattack. Daniel's brigade plugged the trenches below Doles, Brigadier General James A. Walker's Stonewall Brigade held firm to the north, and Brigadier General George H. "Maryland" Steuart's brigade sprinted over from the salient's far side. Then Battle's Alabamians and Brigadier General Robert D. Johnston's North Carolinians dove in, along with Colonel Clement A. Evans's Georgians. Within minutes, Upton's men had been battered back and driven to

A volley spewed from the Rebel works, then another. Gaps appeared in Upton's formation, but the men kept on, clawing through the abatis and over the entrenchments.

ONCE THE ARMY OF THE POTOMAC'S COMMANDER, AMBROSE BURNSIDE RETURNED TO VIRGINIA IN 1864 AS HEAD OF THE INDEPENDENT NINTH CORPS. HIS TIMID ATTACKS AT WILDERNESS AND SPOTSYLVANIA LOST HIM GRANT'S CONFIDENCE AND ULTIMATELY LED TO HIS REPLACEMENT.

(LC)

seek shelter against the outer face of the earthworks.

Upton cast about in vain for the support that he had been promised. Mott, however, had already been repulsed, and Warren's soldiers were too jaded from their earlier attacks against Laurel Hill to help. A few Second and Fifth Corps units ventured into the Spindle fields and momentarily breached Anderson's lines, but their gains were fleeting. "Fruitless as the first," a Federal called the attack. As darkness fell, Upton ordered his men back. "Bitter were the reproaches to which both Russell and Upton gave utterance when upon Upton's return he gained shelter of the woods," a Northerner recounted. "I sat down in the woods," a soldier wrote, "and as I thought of the desolation and misery about me, my feelings overcame me and I cried like a little child."

Although Grant did not realize it, his best opportunity for success on May 10 lay in front of Burnside. Lee had weakened his eastern flank by sending Mahone and Heth to the Po. During the afternoon, a single Confederate division—Cadmus Wilcox's—guarded the Fredericksburg Road, and a yawning gap separated Wilcox from Ewell in the salient. With Sheridan off on his raid, Grant was deprived of his "eyes and ears" and hence missed the opportunity that he had been seeking.

Burnside advanced timidly along the Fredericksburg Road around six o'clock, met determined resistance from Wilcox, and decided to entrench a quarter of a mile from the hamlet. Headquarters then

fretted that Burnside was too far advanced and ordered him back to the Ni. As Grant conceded in his memoirs, withdrawing Burnside "lost to us an important advantage." Even Burnside's soldiers were perplexed. "It was a profound mystery to the men in the ranks, at the time, why such a movement should have been made," a Northerner wrote.

But Grant remained optimistic as ever. Upton had failed, but perhaps the attack held an important lesson. Lee's works were not invulnerable. They could be breached if the attackers moved quickly, without pausing to fire and reload. Upton had failed because he had lacked proper support. What if an attack were launched similar to Upton's with an entire corps? And what if the supporting troops consisted of the rest of the Union army? Here, Grant concluded, lay the key to destroying Lee.

MAY 11: GRANT PREPARES FOR THE GRAND ASSAULT

During the morning of May 11, Grant matured his plans. He decided to spear-

MAJOR GENERAL HORATIO G. WRIGHT TOOK COMMAND OF THE UNION SIXTH CORPS AFTER SEDGWICK'S DEATH ON MAY 9.

(LC)

head the attack with the Second Corps and ordered Hancock to the Brown house, where Mott had launched his charge on the tenth. From there, Hancock was to assault the Confederate salient's tip shortly before daylight on the twelfth. At the same time, Burnside was to attack the salient's eastern leg, and Warren and Wright were to keep the Confederates on Laurel Hill pinned in place. One of Meade's aides summarized the scheme as a "repetition of Mott's attack on the 10th, on a much larger scale in every way."

As the day progressed, Lee received intelligence that Grant might be planning to retire toward Fredericksburg. The Confederate commander wanted to be ready to strike immediately and directed his corps commanders to prepare to march on short notice. He was concerned, however, that artillery in the salient might have difficulty pulling out and hence slow the army's response. According to one of Lee's aides, "orders were given to withdraw the artillery from the salient occupied by Major General Edward "Allegheny" Johnson's division to have it available for a counter-move to the right." Little did Lee suspect that he was weakening the very place that Grant intended to attack.

In the afternoon, rain began falling in torrents. "The wind was raw and sharp," a Federal wrote, "our clothing wet, and we were just about as disconsolate and miserable a set of men as were ever seen."

After dark, Hancock's corps began shifting to the Brown house. The march

was a miserable affair. Soldiers sloshed behind one another and tried to follow their file leader "not by sight or touch, but by hearing him growl and swear, as he slipped, splashed, and tried to pull his 'pontoons' out of the mud." The situation at the Brown house was discouraging. No one seemed to know where the Confederates were or how their line was oriented. Barlow, whose division was to lead the assault, inquired, "What is the nature of the ground over which I have to pass?" He was told, "We do not know." He asked, "What obstructions am I to meet, if any?" only to be told, "We do not know." Exasperated, he demanded, "Have I a gulch a thousand feet deep to cross?" The answer came back, "We do not know." According to one account, an officer drew a rough map on the Brown house wall to show Hancock how to face his troops.

The Second Corps assembled behind Mott's pickets along a compass line drawn from the Brown place to the McCoull house. Barlow's division packed tightly into two lines, Birney on Barlow's right,

WINFIELD HANCOCK (SEATED) AND HIS DIVISION COMMANDERS FRANCIS BARLOW, DAVID BIRNEY, AND JOHN GIBBON.

(LC)

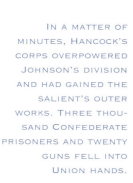

Mott and Gibbon behind. "We thus formed a huge sledge hammer," one of Barlow's officers explained, "of which our division was the head and Birney's the handle," with the remainder of the corps in support. Across the way, Lee's pickets heard sounds—a "subdued roar or noise, plainly audible in the still, heavy night air like distant falling water or machinery"—but were uncertain whether the Federals were leaving or preparing to attack. By midnight, "Allegheny" Johnson, whose division occupied the tip of the salient, concluded that mischief was afoot and dispatched an aide to Ewell asking that the artillery be returned. Ewell rebuffed the staffer, so Johnson visited Ewell himself. The corps

commander was persuaded by Johnson's entreaties and ordered the guns returned. His instructions, however, were inexplicably delayed and failed to reach the artillerists until 3:30 A.M. Rebel gunners ran to their horses and began hauling their pieces through mud toward the salient.

Four o'clock arrived. It was still pitch black, so Hancock postponed the assault for another half hour. A soldier recalled that the men, "surrounded by the silence of night, by darkness and fog, stood listening to the raindrops as they fell from leaf to leaf." At 4:30, the rain stopped and was replaced by a swirling, clinging mist. "Forward!" came the command, and twenty thousand blue-clad soldiers heaved forward. Over the Rebel picket line they pushed and onto a shallow ridge. The sight ahead was daunting. "The red earth of a well defined line of works loomed up through the mists on the crest of another ridge, distant about two hundred yards with a shallow ravine between," a Northerner recounted. Scarcely pausing,

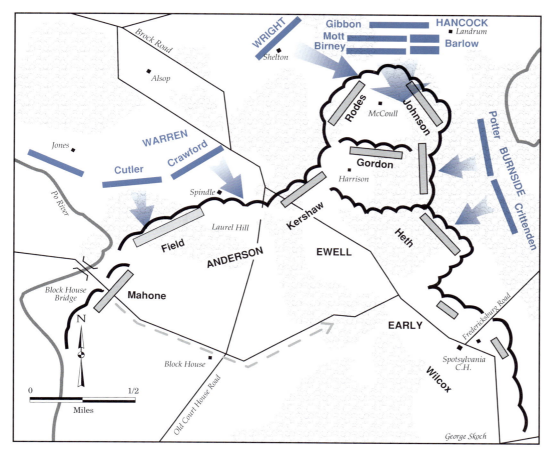

THE BATTLE FOR THE BLOODY ANGLE: MAY 12
At 4:35 A.M., Hancock attacks the Muleshoe Salient, supported by Burnside, on his left, and by Warren, on his right. Hancock annihilates Johnson's division and seizes the salient, but his troops recoil in the face of Confederate counterattacks. Wright's Sixth Corps goes to Hancock's assistance at 6 A.M., but is unable to make any additional headway. A bloody standoff develops.

they dashed into the ravine and up the far side, clawing through abatis. "All line and formation was now lost," a participant recalled, "and the great mass of men, with a rush like a cyclone, sprang upon the entrenchments and swarmed over."

MAY 12: THE ARMIES CONVERGE ON THE BLOODY ANGLE

Hancock obliterated the blunt end of the Confederate salient within minutes. "There was a little pattering of bullets, and I saw a few of our men on the ground," Barlow recounted. "One discharge of artillery, that I remember, and we were up on the works with our hands full of guns,

prisoners, and colors." By most accounts, Confederate resistance was "very slight and ineffectual."

Jones's former brigade, now commanded by Colonel William Witcher, bore the brunt of the attack and was virtually destroyed. Federals lapped around the east edge of the salient and overran "Maryland" Steuart's brigade, capturing both Steuart and Johnson. Dick McClean of Company K, 116th Pennsylvania, took Johnson's sword and led the captured division commander to Hancock. Johnson and Hancock had been close friends before the war. "This is damned bad luck," Johnson exclaimed, "yet I would rather have had this good fortune fall to you than to any other man living." Steuart was not so gen-

Lee's pickets heard sounds—a "subdued roar or noise, plainly audible in the still, heavy night air like distant falling water or machinery"—but were uncertain whether the Federals were leaving or preparing to attack.

THE BLOODY ANGLE:
A UNION PERSPECTIVE

By 6 A.M., May 12, the two armies had reached a stalemate. Hancock's Second Corps had broken the Confederate line but had not been able to push beyond the face of the Muleshoe salient. The Confederates, by like token, had stopped Hancock's progress but had been unable to expel him from the outer works. At 6 A.M., Grant ordered in the Sixth Corps to break the impasse. For the next twenty hours, the fighting would center around a small turn in the Confederate line thereafter known as the "Bloody Angle." G. Norton Galloway, a Union soldier serving in the 95th Pennsylvania Infantry regiment, described the fighting at the Angle in vivid detail.

"The rain was still falling in torrents and held the country about in obscurity. The command was soon given to my regiment, the 95th Pennsylvania Volunteers . . . to 'rise up,' whereupon with hurrahs we went forward, cheered on by Colonel Upton . . . . It was not long before we reached an angle of works constructed with great skill. Immediately in our front an abatis had been arranged consisting of limbs and branches interwoven into one another, forming footlocks of the most dangerous character. But there the works were, and over some of us went many never to return. At this moment Lee's strong line of battle . . . appeared through the rain, mist, and smoke. We received their bolts, losing nearly one hundred of our gallant 95th. Colonel Upton saw at once that this point must be held at all hazards; for if Lee should recover the angle, he would be enabled to sweep back our lines right and left, and the fruits of the morning's victory would be lost. The order was at once given us to lie down and commence firing; the left of our regiment rested against the works, while the right, slightly refused, rested upon an elevation in front. An now began a desperate and pertinacious struggle.

Upon reaching the breastwork, the Confederates for a few moments had the advantage of us, and made good use of their rifles. Our men went down by the score; all the artillery horses were down; the gallant Upton was the only mounted officer in sight. Hat in hand, he bravely cheered his men, and begged them to 'hold this point.' All of his staff had been either killed, wounded, or dismounted.

At this moment . . . a section of Battery C, 5th United States Artillery, under Lieutenant Richard Metcalf, was brought into action and increased the carnage by opening at short range with double charges of canister. This staggered the apparently exultant enemy. In the maze of the moment these guns were run up by hand close to the famous Angle, and fired again and again, and they were only abandoned when all the drivers and cannoneers had fallen. The battle was now at white heat . . . .

Finding that we were not to be driven back, the Confederates began to use more discretion, exposing themselves but little, using the loop-holes in their works to fire through, and at time placing the muzzles of their rifles on the top logs, seizing the trigger and small of the stock, and elevating the breech with one hand sufficiently to reach us. During the day a section of Cowan's battery took position

erous. When Hancock offered his hand and inquired, "How are you, Steuart?" the Rebel general replied, "Under the circumstances, I decline to take your hand." Hancock snapped back, "And under any other circumstances I should not have offered it."

Birney's division advanced on Barlow's right and chewed into the portion of the salient manned by William Monaghan's Louisianians and Walker's Stonewall Brigade. Resistance was more determined, and a Northerner explained that there "ensued one of those hand-to-hand encounters with clubbed rifles, bayo-

behind us, sending shell after shell close over our heads, to explode inside the Confederate works. In like manner Coehorn mortars eight hundred yards in our rear sent their shells with admirable precision gracefully curving over us. Sometimes the enemy's fire would slacken, and the moments would become so monotonous that something had to be done to stir them up. Then some resolute fellow would seize a fence-rail or piece of abatis, and, creeping close to the breastworks, thrust it over among the enemy, and then drop on the ground to avoid the volley that was sure to follow. A daring lieutenant in one of our left companies leaped upon the breastworks, took a rifle that was handed to him, and discharged it among the foe. In like manner he discharged another, and was in the act of firing a third shot when his cap flew up in the air, and his body pitched headlong among the enemy.

On several occasions squads of dishearten Confederates raised pieces of shelter-tents above the works as a flag of truce; upon our slacking fire and calling to them to come in, they would immediately jump the breastworks and surrender.

One party of twenty or thirty thus signified their willingness to submit; but owing to the fact that their comrades occasionally took advantage of the cessation to get a volley into us, it was some time before we concluded to give them a chance. With leveled pieces we called to them to come at it. Springing upon the breastworks in a body, they stood for an

instant panic-stricken at the terrible array before them; that momentary delay was the signal for their destruction. While we, with our fingers pressing the trigger, shouted to them to jump, their troops massed in the rear, poured a volley into them, killing or wounding all but a few,

who dropped with the rest and crawled in under our pieces, while we instantly began firing.

The battle, which during the morning raged with more or less violence on the right and left of this position, gradually slackened, and attention was concentrated upon the Angle. So continuous and heavy was our fire that the

head logs of the breastworks were cut and torn until they resembled hickory brooms. Several large oak-trees, which grew just in the rear of the works, were completely gnawed off by our converging fire, and about 3 o'clock in the day fell among the enemy with a loud crash."

FOR SHEER SAVAGERY, THE FIGHTING AT THE BLOODY ANGLE WAS NEVER SURPASSED. GENERAL L. A. GRANT WROTE, "MEN MOUNTED THE WORKS AND WITH MUSKETS RAPIDLY HANDED THEM KEPT UP A CONTINUOUS FIRE UNTIL THEY WERE SHOT DOWN, WHEN OTHERS WOULD TAKE THEIR PLACES."

(BL)

nets, swords, and pistols which defies description." Another Yankee called the opposition "fanatical." Rebels in the Stonewall Brigade found that their powder was too damp to fire but nonetheless fought "like demons." According to a witness, "the figures of the men seen dimly through the smoke and fog seemed almost gigantic, while the woods were lighted by the flashing of the guns and the sparkling of the musketry." Another retained a vivid image of "men in crowds with bleeding limbs, and pale, pain-stricken faces."

After gobbling up the Stonewall Brigade, Hancock's corps spread south

along the salient's western leg. Daniel's North Carolinians and units from Evans's Georgia brigade braced for the onslaught.

Hancock had torn a gaping hole through the salient. Surprisingly, however, no one had planned the next step. As thousands upon thousands of blue-clad soldiers jammed through an opening no more than three-quarters of a mile wide, all semblance of organization evaporated. The Union Second Corps dissolved into a milling mob. "The enthusiasms of a broken line resulting from victory is only a little more efficient than the despondency of one broken by defeat," an observer remarked. "The officers commanding the divisions were capable men and knew what the situation demanded, but they were almost powerless."

Faced with disaster, Lee's junior officers reacted with boldness and initiative. John Gordon was near a reserve line between the McCoull and Harrison homes when the Union juggernaut struck. Gordon immediately ordered Johnston's North Carolina brigade into the gap created by Steuart's collapse. Working blindly ahead—

"Not a word did he say," a witness recounted, "but simply took off his hat, and as he sat on his charger I never saw a man look so noble, or a spectacle so impressive." Another reminisced: "The picture he made, as the grand old man sat there on his horse, with his noble head bare, and looked from right to left, as if to meet each eye that flashed along the line, can never be forgotten by a man that stood there." As had happened a few days earlier at Widow Tapp's field, Lee

"the mist and fog were so heavy that it was impossible to see farther than a few rods," Gordon later explained—Johnston careered into the Federals. He fell wounded, but Gordon rallied the Carolinians into a thin line bridging Steuart's and Witcher's ruptured works. In the fog and confusion, Gordon's audacity paid off. At tremendous cost—"one of the bloodiest scenes in the war," a soldier called it—Johnston's troops stemmed the breakthrough.

Gordon meanwhile collected Colonel John S. Hoffman's brigade and a portion of Evans's. Lee watched as they fell into line.

spurred his horse Traveller toward the Federals, but the men refused to charge unless he came back. "You must go to the rear," Gordon insisted, and soldiers took up the chant, "Lee to the rear. Lee to the rear." Satisfied that Gordon's men would do their utmost without him, Lee did as they asked.

Gordon advanced "double quick into the vortex of battle" and charged Hancock's masses—"packed thick as blackbirds in our trenches," a Rebel recounted. After half an hour of bruising combat, he had recovered most of the salient's eastern leg.

Major General Robert E. Rodes meanwhile stirred his men to gallant action along the salient's western leg. "Check the enemy's advance and drive them back!" he barked to Stephen Ramseur's crack North Carolina brigade. Ramseur formed his men under a leaden hail of shot and shell and ordered them into the breach. He looked, a soldier thought, "like an angel of war." A correspondent recorded that "so close was the fighting there, for a time, that the fire of friend and foe rose up rattling in one common roar." Taking tremendous casualties, Ramseur's brigade fought toward the Stonewall Brigade's former entrenchments. "Onward over all intervening obstacles," a survivor described their bloody progress. "Onward thro' hissing shot and screaming shell—onward towards the already wavering enemy—onward now after their broken columns—onward into the regained intrenchments." After securing a lodgment in the works, Ramseur began a grueling advance along the salient toward Gordon, one traverse at a time, in an effort to close the gap. His arm dangled at his side from a painful wound.

Grant's response was to send in more troops. Brigadier General Thomas H. Neill's Sixth Corps division headed for the angle where the blunt end of the salient turned south. Referred to in battle accounts as the west angle, it soon earned the popular—and appropriate—appellation of the "Bloody Angle."

First one of Neill's brigades under Colonel Oliver Edwards joined the fray. "It was a life or death contest," a combatant recounted as they packed tightly against the outer face of the west angle in support of Mott. Then two more brigades pitched in. "The spurts of dirt were as constant as the pattering drops of a summer shower,"

THE BLOODY ANGLE: A CONFEDERATE PERSPECTIVE

*A*mong the Confederate regiments holding the Bloody Angle was the First South Carolina Volunteers, one of five regiments in Brigadier General Samuel McGowan's brigade. J. F. J. Caldwell, a twenty-six-year-old lieutenant in the regiment, has left us a detailed description of the Bloody Angle fighting from the Southern standpoint in his book, *A History of a Brigade of South Carolinians.*

"The 12th of May broke cool and cloudy. Soon after dawn a fine mist set in, which sometimes increased to a hard shower, but never entirely ceased, for twenty-four hours.

About ten o'clock, our brigade was suddenly ordered out of the works, detached from the rest of the division, and marched back from the line, but bearing towards the left. The fields were soft and muddy, the rains quite heavy. Nevertheless, we hurried on, often at the double quick. Before long, shells passed over our heads, and musketry became plainly audible in front. Our pace was increased to a run. Turning to the right, as we struck an interior line of works, we bore directly for the firing.

We were now along Ewell's line. The shell came thicker and nearer, frequently striking close at our feet, and throwing mud and water high into the air. The rain continued. As we panted up the way, Maj. Gen. Rodes, of Ewell's corps, walked up to the roadside, and asked what troops we were. 'McGowan's South Carolina brigade,' was the reply. 'There are no better soldiers in the world than these!' cried he to some officers about him. We hurried on, thinking more of him and more of ourselves than ever before.

. . . Soon the order was given to advance to the outer line. We did so, with a cheer

a soldier from Maine recalled, "while overhead the swish and hum of the passing bullets was like a swarm of bees." Then Colonel Lewis A. Grant's Vermonters arrived. "For God's sake, Hancock, do not send any more troops in here," a general reportedly beseeched as soldiers jammed the narrow battle front.

Meanwhile, more Confederates streamed into the salient. Two of Mahone's brigades—those of Brigadier Generals Abner Perrin and Nathaniel H. Harris—hurried back from the Po. One of Perrin's men described the scene as "appalling." He added: "The field was covered with fugitives, some of the artillery was rushing headlong to the rear, and it looked as if some dreadful catastrophe had happened or was about to happen to the army." Perrin's troops advanced through a deadly gauntlet of artillery and musketry— "a very river of death," an Alabamian called it. Perrin was killed, but his troops joined Ramseur's near the angle. Harris's Mississippians came closely on Perrin's heels. "Never did a brigade go into fiercer battle under greater trials," one of Lee's aides later commented. "Never did a brigade do its work more nobly."

By 8:00 A.M., Ramseur, Harris, and Perrin were battling to hold the western face of the west angle. Rain fell in torrents as Confederates fired from inside the works into Federals mere feet away. "The fighting was horrible," a Mississippian recalled. "The breastworks were slippery with blood and rain, dead bodies lying underneath half trampled out of sight."

But still Lee and Grant pumped troops into the Bloody Angle. Brigadier General Samuel McGowan and his South Carolinians dashed for the gap. A soldier recalled shells "bespattering us with dirt, and at the double quick, plunging through mud knee deep, and getting in as best we could. Here, however, lay Harris' Mississippi brigade. We were ordered to close to the right. We moved by the flank up the works, under the fatally accurate fire of the enemy, and ranged ourselves in the entrenchment. The sight we encountered was not calculated to encourage us. The trenches, dug on the inner side, were almost filled with water. Dead men lay on the surface of the ground and in the pools of water. The wounded bled and groaned, stretched or huddled in every attitude of pain. The water was crimsoned with blood. Abandoned knapsacks, guns and accoutrements, with ammunition boxes, were scattered all around. In the rear, disabled caissons stood and limbers of guns. The rain poured heavily, and an incessant fire was kept upon us from front and flank. The enemy still held the works on the right of the angle, and fired across the traverses. Nor were these foes easily seen. They barely raised their heads above the logs, at the moment of firing. It was plainly a question of bravery and endurance now.

We entered upon the task with all our might. Some fired at the line lying in front, on the edge of the ridge before described; others kept down the enemy lodged in the traverses on the right. At one or two places, Confederates and Federals were only separated by the works, and the latter not a few times reached their guns over and fired right down upon the heads of the former . . . .

The firing was astonishingly accurate all along the line. No man could raise his shoulders above the works without danger of immediate death. Some of the enemy lay against our works in front. I saw several of them jump over and surrender during relaxations of firing. An ensign of a Federal regiment came right up to us during the 'peace negotiations,' and demanded our surrender. Lieutenant Carlisle, of the Thirteenth regiment, replied that we would not surrender. Then the ensign insisted that, as he had come under a false impression he should be allowed to return to his command. Lieutenant Carlisle, pleased with his composure, consented. But, as he went back, a man, from another part of the line, shot him through the face, and he came and jumped over to us.

This was the place to test individual courage. Some ordinarily good soldiers did next to nothing, others excelled themselves. The question became, pretty plainly, whether one was willing to meet death, not merely to run the chances of it."

crashing down the limbs about us, and the minnie balls [were] whistling around us at a tremendous rate." McGowan fell injured, as did his senior officer, and command devolved on Colonel Joseph N. Brown, who urged the men through mud knee-deep and reddened with gore. They mingled with Harris's Mississippians and began firing into Unionists on the other side of the entrenchments. "You can imagine our situation," a survivor wrote home. "It was almost certain death for a man to put his head above the works."

Around 9:30 A.M., Brigadier General David A. Russell's Sixth Corps division joined the melee. Upton's men attacked the angle, only to be forced back to a nearby depression. A section of Union artillery pushed almost point-blank against the works and began blasting away. Combatants lay plastered against opposite

VOWING TO EMERGE FROM THE BATTLE A LIVE MAJOR GENERAL OR A DEAD BRIGADIER, BRIGADIER GENERAL ABNER PERRIN LED HIS TROOPS INTO BATTLE AT THE SALIENT. AS HIS HORSE LEAPED OVER THE CAPTURED WORKS, A BULLET ENDED HIS LIFE.

(LC)

sides of the earthworks "like leaches." One of Upton's officers complained that "already there were heaps of our dead lying about and impeding our operations." Then Colonel Henry W. Brown's New Jersey Brigade charged just below the

FOR TWENTY HOURS, FIGHTING RAGED AT THE BLOODY ANGLE. A CONFEDERATE SOLDIER SUMMED UP THE SITUATION WHEN HE WROTE, "THE QUESTION BECAME, PRETTY PLAINLY WHETHER ONE WAS WILLING TO MEET DEATH, NOT MERELY TO RUN THE CHANCES OF IT."

(BL)

west angle. Rebel artillery had the Yankees squarely in range. "The next twenty minutes were horribly fatal," a survivor recounted. "The loss was very heavy," another wrote home. "The gallant 15th Regiment is no more a regiment and it brings tears to one's eyes as he looks upon the little band which now gathers around our colors."

By noon, fighting at the Bloody Angle had achieved a grisly equilibrium. Lee labored to prepare a new line a short way back, relying on his soldiers to defend the salient until the new position was ready. All day, dazed combatants fought grimly on. Men stood on their comrades' bodies and fired blindly into masses of enemy mere feet away. Corpses were stamped into mud and riddled with bullets until they were no longer recognizable. Frenzied soldiers jumped onto the works and fired until they were killed; others jammed rifles through nooks and crannies and shot blindly away. So relentless was the slaughter that men

collapsed from exhaustion on top of corpses, only to jolt awake and start killing again. It seemed as though the two armies had embraced one another in a death grip and refused to let go until one of them was annihilated.

MAY 12: WARREN AND BURNSIDE FALTER

While brutal combat raged at the Bloody Angle, Grant tried to step up pressure against the Rebel flanks. Unfortunately for the Union cause, the commanders on the Federal wings proved unable or unwilling to undertake meaningful action.

The Laurel Hill sector was still in Gouverneur Warren's hesitant hands. Toward six in the morning, as Hancock's attack began to falter, Meade advised the Fifth Corps commander to prepare to attack and "do the best you can." At 7:30, Meade informed Warren that Wright needed support and half an hour later issued peremptory orders to "attack immediately with all the force you can." At 8:15, some of Warren's elements began feeling gingerly ahead. "It was the fourth or fifth assault made by our men," Warren's aide Washington A. Roebling explained, "and it is not a matter of surprise that they had lost all spirit for that kind of work; many of them positively refused to go forward as their previous experience had taught them that to do so was certain death on that front."

After half an hour of unproductive sparring, Warren concluded that he could not advance "at present." Meade was in no mood to quibble and directed Warren to attack "at once at all hazards with your whole force, if necessary." Seeing no alternative, Warren directed his division commanders, "Do it," and added: "Don't mind the consequences." At ten o'clock, the Fifth Corps stepped off once again toward

Laurel Hill.

The charge was a disaster. Advancing near Brock Road, Griffin's division was caught in a "slaughter pen," as one of its members called the Spindle clearing. "Foolishness," complained another. Cutler's division descended into a ravine and came under blistering fire at the Rebel abatis. "In

less than fifteen minutes after we became engaged the ravine lay full of dead men," a survivor recalled. Another declared the movement "almost a farce for we scarcely got but a few paces beyond our lines." A soldier from the famed Iron Brigade wrote home that "Gettysburg is a skirmish compared to this fight."

Headquarters looked poorly on Warren's inaction. "Warren seems reluctant to assault," Meade wrote Grant, who responded, "If Warren fails to attack promptly, send Humphreys to command his corps, and relieve him." Apparently Humphreys handled the matter with tact and assumed responsibility for the Fifth Corps' withdrawal. Warren's standing with his superiors, however, was severely compromised. Shortly before noon, Meade began ordering Warren's subordinates to other parts of the field. Consideration of an offensive against Laurel Hill was abandoned.

Burnside began the day on the other Union flank with a flurry of activity. Before daylight, Brigadier General Robert B. Potter's division stepped into foggy dark-

ness toward the Confederate salient's eastern leg. Potter struck immediately below Steuart's brigade and materially assisted Hancock's break-through. However, Brigadier General James H. Lane's North Carolina brigade had formed below Steuart and resisted Potter's advance. Then more Rebels came to Lane's assistance. "It seemed to us that the dire experience of the Wilderness was about to be repeated," a Northerner explained. "The lurid flash of musketry lighted up the dim woods, and the din of battle resounded on every side."

Lane petitioned his superior—Cadmus Wilcox—for reinforcements, and soon Brigadier Generals Edward L. Thomas's Georgians and Alfred M. Scales's North Carolinians huffed into view. "We crossed our breastworks and advanced several hundred yards under a terrible fire of grape, canister shells and minnie balls," a Confederate recounted. Federals rolled corpses into piles for protection. But neither side could make headway, and for several hours the Ninth Corps remained stymied.

Toward two o'clock in the afternoon, Lee and Grant each looked to Burnside's sector to renew the offensive. Grant sensed opportunity to strike a thinly protected portion of the Confederate line, while Lee correspondingly saw an opening to capture a stand of Ninth Corps cannon that were enfilading Lane. Apparently Orlando Willcox's Federals and Lane's Confederates

started at about the same time. Lane's troops, supported by Weisiger's Virginians, sliced into the advancing Federal column's flank. Neither side was able to make headway in the confused bout of fighting that sputtered through the deep woods.

MAY 13: THE ARMIES ASSESS THE FIGHT AT THE BLOODY ANGLE

Combat continued unabated at the Bloody Angle all day and into the night. Not until 4:00 A.M. on May 13 did Lee inform his troops holding the salient that the new earthworks had been completed. Unit by unit, the exhausted gray-clad troops retired to new fortifications behind the Harrison house.

The sun rose on May 13 over a frightful scene. A soldier from New York wrote his parents that "we have fought one of the greatest battles ever fought. Neither party has been yet badly beaten, though I

think the Johnnies have had the worst of it." Curious to examine the battlefield, he wandered into the salient, now in Union hands. Bodies sprawled everywhere. "The rifle pits were literally chocked with them," he observed, "some of them still breathing." He tried to explain his emotions to his family. "My feelings while looking at the bodies of our dead enemies were not of joy alone," he wrote. "I thought of how many hopes were bound up in the lives of those men whose broken bodies were lying helpless on that muddy field. I had no enmity towards those men, not even any for their living companions who from the woods beyond were even then occasionally sending a whistling bullet after us. They are brave and believe in the cause they fight for."

Grant's aide Horace Porter viewed May 12's handiwork in dismay. "Our own killed were scattered over a large space near the 'angle,'" he recounted, "while in front of the captured breastworks the enemy's dead, vastly more numerous than our own, were piled upon each other in some places four layers deep, exhibiting every ghastly phase of mutilation." He added that "below the mass of fast-decaying corpses, the convulsive twitching of limbs and the writhing of bodies showed that there were wounded men still alive and struggling to extricate themselves from their horrid entombment."

Lee's artillery chief Brigadier General William N. Pendleton wrote his daughter that "in general, we have been quite successful against General Ulysses." He conceded that "by accident night before last, however, they gained an advantage which will partially encourage them." The loss of the salient, he explained, "is the only mishap of consequence," and he went on

to conclude that "no army in the world was ever in finer condition after two days continuous fighting." Captain T. J. Linebarger gave his family a more candid appraisal. "Grant is not like other Yankees," he warned. "Half such a whipping would have sent McClellan, Hooker, Burnside, or Meade crossing to the other side of the Rappahannock, but Grant may join us in battle at any moment." As Captain Linebarger assessed the situation, "It seems that Grant is determined to sacrifice his army or destroy Lee's."

MAY 13–16: GRANT REORIENTS HIS LINE

Once again, Grant had made a determined effort to break Lee's line and failed. And once again, he refused to consider his setback a defeat. He remained true to his strategic goal of applying unrelenting pressure against the Army of Northern Virginia until it snapped. While his soldiers gathered spoils from the battlefield on May 13, Grant laid the groundwork for a major shift, planning to move the Fifth and Sixth Corps behind the Second and past Burnside's left flank. His goal was to mass his forces near the eastern approaches to Spotsylvania and renew battle there.

Weary Northerners slogged all night through a drenching downpour. "The mud was deep over a large part of the route," an aide observed. "The darkness was intense, so that literally you could not see

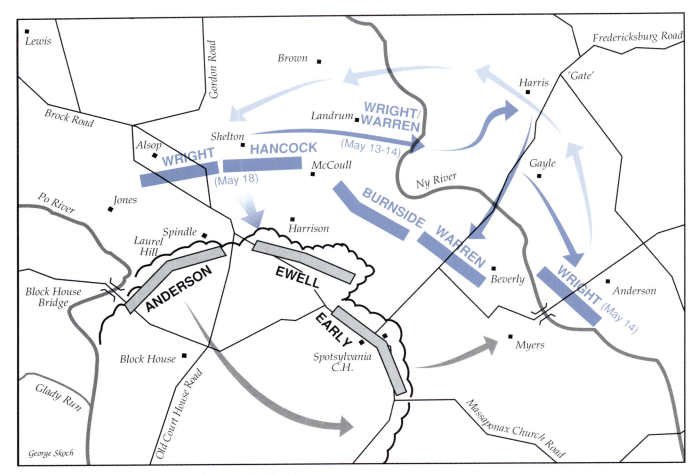

GRANT MANEUVERS FOR POSITION: MAY 13–18

In the wake of the Bloody Angle fighting, Lee withdraws Ewell's corps to a new line below the Harrison House. On the night of May 13, Grant begins sidling the army to the left, across the Fredericksburg Road, resulting in a fight for Myers Hill. When Lee counters by shifting Anderson's corps to the right, Grant orders Hancock and Wright to attack the Confederate line below the Harrison House, hoping to catch Lee out of position. Hancock and Wright find the Confederates firmly in place, however, and their May 18 attacks are easily repulsed.

your hand held before your face." Early the next morning, elements from Ayres's brigade occupied Myers' Hill west of the Fredericksburg Road and below the Ni. The position overlooked much of the Rebel line and anchored Grant's flank. Upton reached the hill shortly, and hot little skirmishes flared around the elevation all day. Hindered by miserable roads and his soldiers' exhausted condition, Meade could not organize an assault against Spotsylvania. The army, an aide remarked, was "broken and scattered and it was not practicable to get the command in condition for offensive operations that day."

In point of fact, Grant had again missed a golden opportunity. Lee had been slow to apprehend Grant's shift and had left the courthouse hamlet lightly guarded. Toward day's end, however, he realized Grant's intentions and shifted part of the First Corps to Spotsylvania Court House. By May 15, Grant's line ran roughly north to south, from the Landrum house to a point past Myers' Hill. Lee's army stretched from behind the former salient across the Fredericksburg Road and on to Snell's Bridge below Spotsylvania Court House.

"We have had five days' almost constant rain without any prospect yet of its clearing up," Grant explained to Washington. "All offensive operations necessarily cease until we can have twenty-four hours of dry weather." A Confederate informed his family that "you can hardly imagine how uncomfortable we are lying in the mud." He added that "for nearly two weeks our men have been in line of battle —exposed to all the inclemency of weather—first the insufferable heat and now the drenching rains—and yet they stand and fight." He closed with a heartfelt plea. "I am worn out and wearied in mind, with continued anxiety. Oh if it could all end, and this terrible turmoil cease!"

MAY 17–18: GRANT TESTS LEE AGAIN

On May 17, the Virginia sun finally peeked from behind the clouds. Soldiers hung their clothes out to dry and Grant pondered where to strike next. One school of thought held that Grant's buildup along the Fredericksburg Road must have induced Lee to weaken his line near the former salient. Grant found this argument persuasive and ordered the Second and Sixth Corps to attack there at sunrise the next morning. During the night, Hancock's men retraced their steps to the Landrum house, across from the Bloody Angle. By 4:00 A.M., they had formed to attack, supported by Sixth Corps elements to the right and Ninth Corps elements to the left.

Ewell's troops occupied the opposing works and had used the rainy interlude to perfect their entrenchments. In front of their position spread an extensive clearing, strewn with abatis and dominated by artillery. And this time, unlike on the twelfth, Ewell was ready. Blue-clad soldiers swarmed into the clearing to a now familiar story. Abatis and entanglements pinned them in place while Ewell's artillery blistered the field with a devastating barrage. The charge was destroyed by ordnance

alone. Afterward, Confederate foot soldiers congratulated the artillerists and affectionately patted their guns.

Lee's decisive repulse of Hancock persuaded Grant to seek a new field of combat. As he had done after the Wilderness, Grant resorted to maneuver to extract Lee from his near impregnable position. Hancock was to march to the rail line between Fredericksburg and Richmond, then turn south. Grant hoped that Lee would follow. "If the enemy make a general move to meet this," Grant explained, "they will be followed by the three other corps . . . and attacked if possible before time is given to entrench."

GENERAL ULYSSES S. GRANT

(NA)

MAY 19: EWELL STUMBLES AT HARRIS'S FARM

Before Grant could spring his trap, Lee seized the initiative by sending Ewell on a reconnaissance in force to locate Grant's northern flank. On the afternoon of May 19, Ewell took the larger part of

ON MAY 18 GRANT STRUCK AT THE BASE OF THE MULESHOE. EWELL'S MEN, FIGHTING BEHIND EARTHWORKS LIKE THESE, EASILY REPULSED THE ATTACK.

(LC)

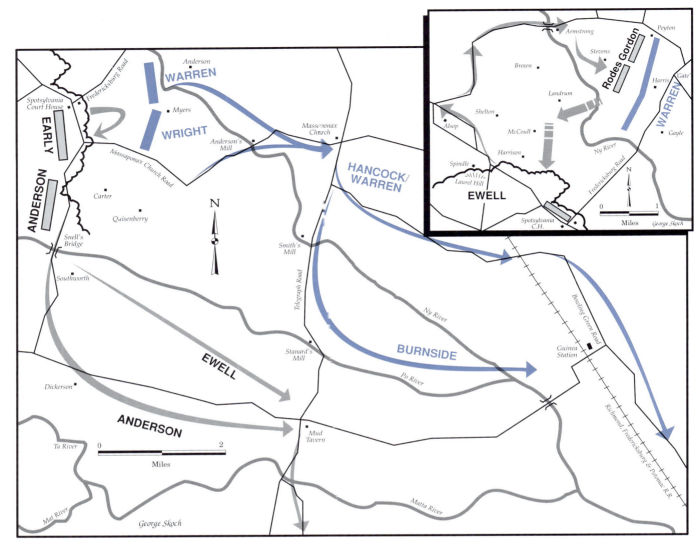

THE ARMIES ABANDON SPOTSYLVANIA: May 21

Unable to crack Lee's entrenched line at Spotsylvania, Grant determines to pry him out of position by dispatching Hancock's corps to Milford Station. Before he can implement this plan, however, Ewell leads his depleted corps in a reconnaissance toward the Fredericksburg Road, resulting in a sharp fight on May 19 at the Harris farm (inset). When Ewell falls back to his previous position, Hancock starts for Milford Station, compelling Lee to abandon Spotsylvania and retreat south along the Telegraph Road.

Rodes's and Gordon's divisions up Brock Road, past corpses moldering on the Spindle field, then northeast on the Gordon Road toward Fredericksburg. Around five o'clock that afternoon, he stumbled upon several heavy artillery regiments serving as infantry. For some of the "Heavies," this was their first exposure to combat. As fighting heated up, they were reinforced by the First Maryland returning from furlough. Meade pumped Birney's division into the fray, and a confused and bitter round of combat ensued.

Lee became increasing concerned as Ewell became drawn into a major engagement far from the rest of the army. When firing sputtered out around 9:00 P.M., Ewell's soldiers immediately began working their way back to their former position. Many lost their way and were captured. The engagement at Harris's farm was a pointless and costly skirmish, and the "Heavies" had acquitted themselves well. Ewell lost over nine hundred men collecting intelligence that a cavalry squad could just as well have gathered.

EPILOGUE

On May 21, Grant initiated his shift south that had been delayed by the Harris farm escapade. For the next few weeks, the armies maneuvered toward Richmond, Grant seeking an opening and Lee deftly blocking him at every turn. First Grant marched to the North Anna, only to discover that Lee had arrived first and was busy erecting more devilish earthworks. Then he sidestepped to the Totopotomy, where Lee again drew a firm line. After more deployments, the armies clashed at Cold Harbor. Temporarily stymied, Grant broke the deadlock by shifting across the James to Petersburg. And there the dance of maneuver that began in the Wilderness ended as the armies settled into siege.

Casualties in the opening battles of the spring campaign cannot be given with certainty. Grant's casualties in the Wilderness amounted to about 18,000, and another 18,400 at Spotsylvania, for a total in killed, wounded, and captured of roughly 36,400. Attrition also gutted Grant's top leadership. Of his four infantry corps heads, one lay dead and two others—Warren and Burnside—seemed incapable of performing acceptably. Even Hancock, generally touted as Grant's ablest subordinate, made amateurish mistakes. He permitted Sorrel to flank him in the Wilderness, nearly lost Barlow below the Po, and lost control of his troops during the attack on the salient.

Three Union division heads were killed or disabled, and fifteen brigade commanders became casualties. According to the Army of the Potomac's medical director, 434 Union officers were wounded in the Wilderness alone.

Lee lost close to 11,000 soldiers killed, wounded, or captured in the Wilderness; his subtractions at Spotsylvania were approximately 10,200 soldiers, for a grand total of 21,200 troops lost from May 4 through 21. The battles also took a severe toll on Lee's command. Two of his three infantry corps heads were disabled, a division commander was captured, and fifteen brigade commanders were killed, captured, or severely wounded. Regiments and companies were decimated. And on May 11, Jeb Stuart received a mortal wound at Yellow Tavern. The Army of Northern Virginia's capacity to undertake offensive operations was quickly disappearing.

The Wilderness and Spotsylvania operations stand among the most fascinating episodes in American military history. In these initial encounters, Lee and Grant each exhibited strengths, and each fumbled. Grant, unlike Lee, did not exercise direct control over his army, but rather had to go through Meade and Burnside. The awkward command hierarchy shackled Grant and thwarted his ability to execute tactical combinations. The popular perception of Grant is that of a general who eschewed maneuver and blindly hurled

The Wilderness and Spotsylvania operations stand among the most fascinating episodes in American military history. In these initial encounters, Lee and Grant each exhibited strengths, and each fumbled.

THE FIRST MAINE HEAVY ARTILLERY TOOK 481 CASUALTIES AT THE HARRIS FARM, BY FAR THE MOST SUSTAINED BY ANY REGIMENT IN THE CAMPAIGN.

(NPS)

men against impregnable earthworks. His record in the Wilderness and Spotsylvania does not bear out that image. He began the campaign by maneuvering Lee from his Rapidan works, then concentrated against Lee's weakest link on May 6 and almost succeeded. On May 7 when it was apparent that Lee held a strong position, Grant again resorted to maneuver and tried to draw Lee south. His combinations on May 10, 12, and 18 represented different methods of trying to crack Lee's line. Grant failed, not because his ideas were faulty, but rather because his subordinates seemed incapable of executing coordinated movements in a timely fashion. Perhaps history will come to judge Grant's failure to take control of the Army of the Potomac and the Ninth Corps with a firm hand early in the campaign as his chief shortcoming.

A troubling aspect of Grant's generalship in the Wilderness, and more so at Spotsylvania, was his tendency to undertake offensive operations before he had fully thought through the next step. On the evening of May 9, he impetuously ordered Hancock over the Po; a more reasoned approach would have been to defer the move until the next morning, thereby preserving the element of surprise. The attack against the Bloody Angle serves as a case in point. It was undertaken on short notice with no clear idea about where to attack or what obstacles would be encountered

Most surprisingly, Grant never seems to have considered what had to be done after Hancock punched through Lee's line. The fact that Hancock's vaunted Second Corps, pride of the Union army, dissolved into a throng with no discernible chain of command speaks eloquently about the absence of forethought.

The problems of command that plagued Grant in the Wilderness and Spotsylvania continued throughout the campaign. The general's strong point remained his tenacity. He was undaunted by tactical reverses that would have sent his predecessors packing. Longstreet, who had been best man at Grant's wedding before the war, made an accurate prediction about his friend. "That man will fight us every day and every hour till the end of the war."

Lee, on the other hand, maneuvered his veterans with a practiced hand and engaged in gambles characteristic of his military style. His decision to attack in the Wilderness with two corps, each separated by several miles of thick woods, was risk-taking of the highest order. Superb fighting by Lee's subordinates, along with a large measure of good fortune, produced results that Southerners could proudly call victory. And Lee's masterful shift of Heth and Mahone to the Po on May 9–10 and his response to Hancock's breakthrough on May 12 stand as set pieces in the art of defensive warfare. But some of Lee's decisions, such as his failure to reposition Hill during the night of May 5–6 and his withdrawal of artillery from the salient on May 11, nearly destroyed his army. Despite occasional lapses, however, Lee achieved stunning results against a vastly superior force. His performance in the Wilderness and Spotsylvania places him in the foremost rank of American commanders.